The Narrow Road

MacKenzie Price Myers

Copyright © 2015 by #kwya

All rights reserved.

ISBN-13: 978-1511816960
ISBN-10: 1511816961

"*The Narrow Road* is written from a very real place. The stories that you read are deep and raw and written with brutal honesty about who MacKenzie is at her core. You will find yourself identifying with many parts of this book, and the truths that MacKenzie reveals will bring you to a place of freedom and true identity."

Benjamin Myers
Senior Worship Pastor, Heritage Fellowship

"One of the greatest joys that parents will ever experience is to see their children serving the Lord with passion and zeal. We experience that joy daily as we observe our daughter, MacKenzie. Her abandoned pursuit of God's presence and His design for her life has been creatively and vulnerably shared in her book, *The Narrow Road*. The sharing of her journey will certainly challenge each reader to reflect upon their journeys of life."

Jim Price
Senior Pastor, Heritage Fellowship

DEDICATION

With great love I dedicate this book to my amazing husband and precious daughters. May your feet be always steady on the Narrow Road.

"MacKenzie's journey to knowing who she is in Christ, can provide great insights for all women who struggle with their identity. Though it is very personal and very raw at times, most women can relate to it. I pray that many women will be brave enough to read this book and in doing so, will find their very own personal identity as daughters of the King."

Linda Quesenberry
Prayer Coordinator, Heritage Fellowship

"*The Narrow Road* is a book that, simply put, calls you to find the narrow way and never give up on your journey. Its message is one that challenges you to a deeper walk with the Father. You will be both encouraged and challenged through the many real and genuine stories and testimonies that fill these pages."

Kara Moss
Wife, mother, business owner

"MacKenzie's very honest and vulnerable way of writing about her journey both challenges, and gives us hope, to get beyond the obstacles in our own lives that keep us from being who we really are in Jesus!"

Peggy Price
Worship Arts Pastor, Heritage Fellowship

CONTENTS

Invitation

Where is the Road?	Pg 9
The Gate	Pg 18
Letting Go	Pg 29
I Am Clay	Pg 36
Through the Storm	Pg 49
A Better Way	Pg 64
The Mile-High Pile	Pg 77
Keys	Pg 93
Petals	Pg 110
Bones to Breath	Pg 120
The Treasure of Waiting	Pg 135

INVITATION FROM MACKENZIE

We are about to begin a journey together. It is going to be exciting but also difficult at times. Trying to find truth in this darkened world is not a battle for the faint of heart. It takes strength to surrender and humility to rise. This book is full of stories from my life when the Lord dealt with my heart. I had to learn how to be strong so that I could surrender my life to Christ. I had to learn how to humble myself so that I could rise again and walk the Narrow Road. Now, here I am praying the same for you.

I pray that as Matthew 7:14 begins to work in your heart that you would see clearly what the Road looks like for you. I see the Road as a lifestyle. Once I see the Gate and begin my journey on the Road, my choices in life determine if my feet stay steady or stray. The Road I see is straight, never ending, and beautiful. This book is full of moments in my life when I was learning how to walk the Narrow Road.

Soften your heart and prepare the way for the Lord to come in. As you read my stories, you will see that His Word is woven within them everywhere. I remember reading books as a young girl, and when there was scripture I would skip over it or skim it. In this book, I set His words apart from my own to honor them. If there is one thing that I would plead with you, it is this — please do not pass by His words. They are life and breath, and can soften and change even the most wounded hearts. I pray that my life might encourage yours as you read the pages of this book. I pray from this point on that your steps would be steady, and your eyes fixed on the Road ahead. Whoever you are, I love you with the most beautiful love that comes from Jesus.

Now, we've heard about this Narrow Road — let's be the few that find it!

CHAPTER 1: WHERE IS THE ROAD?

"But small is the gate and narrow the road that leads to life, and only a few find it." Matthew 7:14

Where is the road? We have heard about it for years. We have read the scriptures, heard the teachings, gone to the Bible study… but we still cannot find this Road. The Narrow Road. We feel ashamed to let others know that not only are we not doing a great job of staying on the Road, but we have not even found it yet. As this shame blankets us, it begins to destroy us. We grow bitter because, for some reason, we cannot even find the Gate that takes us to the Road. Obviously, we have to find the Gate before we can find the Road and that in itself seems too difficult. We put on a show of walking the Road without having made the sacrifice to find it.

It is not because of a lack of trying. Not everyone knows this, but as women, we are fighters. We are strong. We do not give up. Every morning we give ourselves that "pep talk". Yeah, you know the one. We set in our hearts to do a better job that day thinking good thoughts, honoring our husbands, loving our children, and having that amazing quiet time with the Lord. In our strength, we fail, and end another day having not found the Road. We go to bed feeling frustrated, being aggravated at the world, and regretting another day wasted.

> *"My guilt overwhelmed me. Like a heavy load, it is more than I can bear." Psalms 38:4*

We lay there choosing to be weighed down by the happenings of that day. We play back every failed moment in our minds. We convince ourselves that we *ARE NOT* good enough, and we *NEVER WILL BE* good enough. But, I am here to tell you that the Bible also says,

> *"Give your burdens to the Lord, and He will take care of you." Psalms 55:22*

We were never meant to walk this journey alone. We were never meant to carry all of our burdens and brokenness alone. Our Heavenly Father will never leave us or forsake us no matter what our days look like or how long our nights are. He is taking our statements and changing a few words to tell us we *ARE* good enough, and we *WILL ALWAYS BE* good enough. It is not our goodness, but His within us. For we are made in His image, and He said that it was very good!

"God created mankind in His own image..." Genesis 1:27

When the Lord made you, when He designed every part of *YOU* personally, He put His fingerprint on you. You are His! We are His! Even though He chose us from the beginning, He still gives us the freedom to choose Him or reject Him. He wants a genuine relationship with us. We have to know that the fingerprint of God is upon our lives. Because of what He did for us on the cross, we become whole. When we say yes to Him, we tap into the *good* that was impregnated in us from creation.

It was there in the garden that we lost our way. We were tempted, and we failed. We gave ear to the spirit of pride, jealousy, and arrogance. We believed what it said. There should be no shame in the temptation. In this world, things will try to grab our attention and pull us away. It is the choice we make after the temptation that sets us apart. We have to try to find our way through the temptations of this world. We have to find our way through the different moods and attitudes that want to come out of our hearts. It is one thing to have the emotion of wanting to yell and snap at my children and another if I follow through with it. The sin is often in the action.

We lose our way by the choices we make. I wonder how many nights Eve went to bed replaying that day over and over in her mind, wondering what she should have done differently to overcome temptation. She was in the Bible, but she was just a woman — a woman like me, a woman like you. Do not think for a second that Eve was perfectly fine with how things went down. No way! She got herself and her husband kicked out of the garden! Because of her they now had to adjust to living in Sin City instead of Paradise Country. I guarantee that she struggled! I guarantee that she fought with herself and did the "how could you" lines that tear us down. She probably had many talks with Adam about the day that forever changed their lives. She probably went through different stages of healing for what she had done.

If you are like me, you will be dealing with an issue, and the Lord will come and do a beautiful healing job. A year later, you find yourself at the next layer ready to be healed at a deeper place within your heart. I believe that you can only receive the amount of healing for the amount of pain you understand and hurt you are willing to release. I believe we are human beings made of layers, and if the wound goes deeply enough, one layer of healing is not enough. God *CAN* heal you from something all at once. He can! He can do anything and everything He wants! However, I find that He does like to work in layers. Working in layers gives us the opportunity to choose again and again to release hurt, to forgive, and to receive forgiveness. This gives us the chance to let the Lord work in us new revelations of our healing process.

I believe that Eve did not say to the Lord and Adam "forgive me" one time and then it was over. I believe she went through stages of releasing the guilt she carried from the choices she made. I believe she asked many times for forgiveness. I am not always sure which is easier, the asking for or the giving of forgiveness. But, both must be done. Letting the Lord work in us is just part of the journey…a journey that leads us to the Narrow Road.

That is all we want, right? We want to get to the Gate! We

want to find the Narrow Road. We want to be that woman of God that others look up to as an example. Sheesh, who are we kidding? Really, we just want to be proud of ourselves. So, how do we get from lost to found? How do we find the Narrow Road in our crazy-making lunch-doing laundry-loving on our husbands-going to work-training our children-taking the trash out kind of lives? Is it even possible? It is not like we have five hours a day to devote to reading the Word and praying. Gosh, we do not even have an hour. We might have ten minutes. "What can we do in ten minutes, Lord?"

If you are carrying the burden of thoughts like that, just let them all go. Be released. Be washed of that mindset. It is not about the number of hours we spend in "quiet time". Having personal time with the Holy Spirit is absolutely important! However, someone could spend twelve hours a day before the Lord and not have found the Road. It is not about performance. It is not about how many hours we give Him. We should be giving Him every hour of our lives. We must have the revelation that He does not just want us to go to church on Sunday and give Him a few minutes every other day. He desires that every minute we are breathing belongs to Him. Our way back to the Road happens when we surrender. If we want to find our way, we must let these words take deep root in our hearts…

"In all your ways submit to Him, and He will make your paths straight." Proverbs 3:6

When we finally let go, surrendering everything we do, and everything we are to Him, He can begin showing us the way. Only in our submission to the Lord can our eyes be open to see the Gate. Surrendering our lives to Christ is more than acknowledging our sin and asking for forgiveness. Yes, we must do that, but that is not the end of our surrender story. Surrender happens every day when we are faced with choices. Do we choose to hold on to our lives, or do we trust that He knows what is best for us?

When we truly surrender, the blinders fall from our eyes, and we find that the Gate is right before us. It has always been there. It has never been far from us. We always felt like the Gate was a journey away and that we would never get to it. We searched aimlessly, looking through eyes that could not see. We kept fighting in our strength to find this Gate and to find our own way. Why does it take us so long to realize that it is in our weakness that He is strong?

> *"My kindness is all you need. My power is strongest when you are weak." 2 Corinthians 12:9*

It is in our blindness that He can bring sight. Why do we ever think we can do it on our own? It is in our humility and surrender that the Lord removes our blinders. For the first time, we see a ray of light. We see hope. We see the Gate.

The Gate is His presence…and His presence is always before us. It is always there for us at any moment we choose to surrender. When we give up the control we think we have, His Spirit begins to minister healing to us, and we find that we can see. Just like the blind man in Luke 18, we must cry out to the Lord! We must be bold! The leaders near the blind man scolded him and told him to be quiet, but he only grew louder. He wanted to *see*. Jesus came close to the man and asked,

> *"What do you want me to do for you?" Luke 18:41*

I think if you listen closely, you will hear your Savior asking you the same question. So, what do you want Him to do? Do you want Him to change your life? Do you want Him to heal your blindness? Then, you must surrender. You must give Him your whole life! When you are ready to surrender and answer honestly, answer like the blind man.

> *"He said, 'Lord, I want to see.' Jesus said to him, 'Receive your sight! Your faith has healed you.' At once he was able to see..." Luke 18:41-43*

Receive your sight! Just like the blind man, have faith and ask the Lord to heal you! He can do it! And all at once you will see the beautiful Gate before you. I remember the exact moment when my spiritual eyes were healed. It was not during a long service at church but in a quiet moment in my home. It felt like I was literally standing in front of the Gate. To my surprise, the Gate of His presence was not grand with gold and jewels. It was humbly made...as if made by a Carpenter. Most anyone looking for the Gate would pass by this one. They would be envisioning a gate of glory for them to pass through in all of their mighty knowledge of God. They would not even see this humble Gate.

How I pray that I am not like one who passes by the real Gate for a gate that would satisfy my flesh! Encountering His presence has nothing to do with how well we know the Bible or how well we can lead worship. It does not matter how well we dance, play an instrument, preach, paint, or play a sport. Finding the Gate of His presence is for the lowly. Finding the Gate cannot be about us. We will walk the rest of our lives blindly if we pursue Him for our own sake and fame. It is *ALL* about Him! Everything! No exceptions!

"For I, the Lord your God, am a jealous God"

Exodus 20:5

He wants it all. He wants every part of us. He gave us His only Son that we might be friends with Him. Why do we so easily forget what He has done for us? Why do we ever think building our own kingdom will satisfy us? Stone by stone, we will only grow more weary and restless. We will find that our vision has died, and we are alone. No one truly wants to help us build a kingdom that is for us. There have been amazing kings and leaders in history, but deep down, we were not created with a desire to build a kingdom for a man. Our soul longs for something eternal. Our soul yearns to build His kingdom.

We have to give up our own plans and our own kingdoms. We have to surrender. It is time to surrender! It is time to acknowledge that nothing else is working, and we are lost. It is time to find our way back. Get away with God even for just a few minutes. He knows your heart. Tell Him how you feel. Open your heart and begin to let Him work. Let Him shape and heal you. Let Him breathe on your eyes and give you sight. Then, just trust. Let go of fear and just trust.

Slowly, open your eyes and see that beautiful, humble Gate right before you. It has been there the whole time. Where is the Road? It is one choice away. When we surrender and live life in His presence, we have found the Narrow Road. Sow your tears into the ground in front of the Gate. Humble yourself, and be filled with a thankful heart. Once you were lost, but now you are found.

CHAPTER 2: THE GATE

What a precious thing it is…to be found. It does not matter how old we get, on the inside we can be as lost as a child in a maze. We are lost with no hope, no joy, and worst of all, no love. It is ridiculous to think we choose a life like that. These feelings may come and go. They may only last a few days, or maybe they last for months at a time. To help us label our issues the world calls it anxiety and depression. I understand that these two things can be very real. I have had to deal with them myself!

There have been days that I did not want to get out of bed. Some days I literally could not breathe, and panic would begin to take over my body. I would feel helpless — helpless and hopeless. I did not want to do anything. It was as if life was constantly being sucked out of me. I would lose sight of everything. I would give myself that pep talk and good counsel, but I would not want to listen.

The Gate

Over and over, I would reach this breaking point only to pull back just in time to cover up my issues and put on a smile. I would never fully let go and surrender to the cross. I would bottle everything up and stuff it until next time — and, every "next time" was just like the time before. Nothing would change, and I would deal with the same things over and over. If we put ourselves on a cycle that goes around and around, how do we ever think that we will move forward? We have to get to a place of holy anger that says, "NO MORE!" No more cycle! No more shutting down! No more hiding! No more anxiety! No more depression! We have to get fed up with the old ways and cry out for a new way of living. When we decide to step out of the cycle and start taking our first steps forward, our whole world is going to be shaken.

I felt my world shaking in October of 2014, and I was not prepared for it. I did not have my armor on in the spirit, and I was crumbling. My family had been praying for a specific breakthrough for many months(years actually), and it was not coming. Typically, I am more optimistic than my husband. I am the one that can look out and see what is not there. I am Mrs. Prophetic. Therefore, I did not get discouraged over the months — or so I thought.

I was the one standing strong, waiting patiently for our breakthrough. All in one week, my issues began surfacing. I realized I had carried bitterness towards the Lord over the months of our praying. I realized I had to deal with past regrets. I realized I had to work on the anger in my heart. It was all too much. I had felt like a strong person up until that week. Suddenly, I felt like there was a crack going from the top of my head down to my feet, and I was just about to fall apart. I felt like I did not know who I was anymore. I felt like the foundation under my feet was crumbling. I would not talk to anyone; I would not even journal about it. I could not. I honestly could not get the words out. I felt alone and frustrated, and I had no idea what to do. I was at the breaking point in the cycle. But finally — finally — I let His holy anger rise within me, and I fought with everything I had not to shrink back into my shell. I did not want to repeat this cycle. I wanted to move forward!

You may think that my righteous anger told me to suck it up, dry my eyes, and stand strong, right? If I did not want to shrink back and repeat the cycle, I needed to do the opposite and be a strong woman. Well, I was a strong woman. I did stand firm. But, standing firm does not always look like the world says it does. I needed to fight — but my fight was to surrender. My surrender was to let Him break everything in me. Because of my isolation, my sister and brother-in-law's love and concern caused them to drop by and check on me. My standing firm looked like falling into their arms. It looked like a fountain of tears as I acknowledged a whole lot of brokenness.

I was thankful for those that the Lord put in my life. I remember that day so well. If it had not been for the Lord using my sister and her husband that day, I might have gone back to my cycle. I was a mess. I was not strong enough to face my hurt and issues on my own, but with them around me, there was extra grace for what needed to be done. They held me and prayed for me, and I felt loved and protected. On that day, I was able to acknowledge my need for Christ in a whole new way.

Isn't that always what our Father is working in us? No matter what the issue is, He always wants to deepen our understanding of how much we need Him. He desires us to want Him as much as He wants us. I do not believe we will ever comprehend His full love for us until we meet Him in our Heavenly home. He gives us a choice. It is the choice of staying in the cycle or of being brave and stepping forward with Him. The more we go through the process, the more He can work in our lives. The Lord works with us in layers. He shows us how deep the wound goes, and we have to acknowledge that hurt in its fullness. He then comforts and heals to that level.

That week in my life He was working on an entirely new level! I was not quite sure how I was going to make it through, but I did not care. It was about full surrender to Him, and I was going to try to walk that out. Even now, I am not far past my breaking point with Him, but I know this is already a better journey than traveling on that same cycle over and over again. It has not been easy, and there are moments that I still want to have a panic attack, but His grace is enough. He is more than I will ever need, and as long as I continue to surrender to Him, He will continue to break things in me and change me. I am thankful to be off the cycle and moving forward.

It is a powerful thing for a woman of God to walk forward in her destiny. The enemy does not want that to happen. Be prepared for him to whisper lies as the attacks come. Guard up!

"Put on the full armor of God so that you can take your stand against the devil's schemes." Ephesians 6:10

I believe this more than ever! As women of God, we must protect ourselves with the armor He gives. I feel a lot of our responses would be different if we lived life wearing our armor. Also, we need to know who we should be fighting. Our fight is not with our husbands, it is not with our children, it is not with our friends and co-workers. We have to be strong in the Lord and put on the armor He has given us. We have to stand against the enemy's plans for our lives.

"For our struggle is not against flesh and blood, but against the rulers, against the authorities, against the powers of this dark world and against the spiritual forces of evil in the heavenly realms." Ephesians 6:11

Depression is a darkness and heaviness that comes and lays itself on us. If we let it, it begins to seep into our beings and make a home in our hearts — in our spirit man. However, we are not "dark" beings. We were created in His image, and He is the

"...Light of the world." John 8:12

Listen to me! I am telling you...

"The night is almost gone, and the day is near. Therefore, let us lay aside the deeds of darkness and put on the armor of light." Romans 13:12

Come on, spirit man! Rise up! Wake up! Let's put on our armor together and stand against this darkness that wants to consume us. I am speaking now over your life that the night you have been living through is almost over! The day is coming! The sun is rising! We *MUST* watch our actions and pursue Christ. We must put on our armor of light and stand firm through the trials.

Sometimes standing firm looks strangely different than how the world would see it. I see a generation of believers who have learned to put on their armor and stand firm as their knees hit the ground, and their hands lift in surrender. Standing firm is about strength of heart, not body. What I have learned that strengthens my heart — my spirit man — more than anything else are the moments at His feet.

Surrender is a powerful tool in our hands. So often, we do not use it, or we only use it halfway. Full surrender can free us! It is this act that begins our process of finding the Narrow Road. It is the first step that allows us to see the Gate that stands before us — the Gate of His presence. How precious. How precious it is to be truly found in our surrender. He sees us. He sees you! You are more important to Him than you could ever imagine. He wanted you, so He made you. He wants you, so He died for you. Christ did not have to create you...but because He *WANTED* you, He formed you in your mother's womb and gave you life! However, today we are separated from God because of the barrier created by sin. Christ did not have to die on the cross...but because He *WANTS* you(forever), He gave His life in order to make a way. He destroyed the barrier! He wants to have a relationship with you! The cross is a symbol of His love! He wants to be your friend. He does not tower over you giving you rules and regulations, but instead, He is giving you a hand to take. He wants you to climb into His lap just like a child would. He is our Dad. He is *your* Dad.

For some of you, you may need to take a few deep breaths. Cry it out. Let the Lord minister the thought of Him being a Dad to you. Some of us have had a wonderful father, and some of us have not. It does not matter what background you come from, we all need our Heavenly Father. We need Him no matter how old we get. Our Heavenly Father is tender and loving, and ready to walk the rest of this journey with us. From the first step of surrender to our very last breath, He is there. I know it may not always seem like that. I have even had my moments of disbelief, but He is just like the Gate. Though we may not have eyes to see, it does not mean it is not there. Do not miss this moment with Him. Stop reading, and let Him minister to you.

Now that we have surrendered, and we can see the Gate, what is next? First, I would say surrender is a process. Because we are always growing and changing, our level of surrender will have to increase as well. We must never get caught up in the thought that we are done with that step. We will have to go the rest of our lives continually surrendering to Him, or we will lose our way, the Gate will disappear, and we will never walk the Narrow Road. I know that sounds harsh, but walking with your Creator costs a high price. It costs your life.

"I have been crucified with Christ, and I no longer live, but Christ lives in me." Galatians 2:20

If you are spending the currency of your life on anything other than Him, you will not have enough to pay the price. Hear my heart. I am being real with you. I am not saying you have to work in a church or ministry or be a missionary. He could call you to be a doctor, lawyer, mechanic, chef, or teacher. No matter what your function is on this earth, you can live it out for the Lord, or you can live it out for yourself and just do the "church" thing.

> *"Whatever you do, work at it with all your heart, as working for the Lord..."* Colossians 3:23

Spend your life on Him. Give Him your family life. Give Him your career. Give Him your free time. Surrender everything, every day. If you mess up, release it to the Lord and keep going.

> *"Therefore, there is now no condemnation for those who are in Christ Jesus."* Romans 8:1

Do not lose heart. Keep pressing in! Our Heavenly Father does not hold our past failures over our head or throw them at us as He pleases. He delights in our success and walks with us through our mistakes. He does not expect us to get everything together on our own or heal our own broken hearts. That is too much for us. We need Him!

We are standing at the Gate, and we need Him. We need Him because we are carrying too much to fit through. Right when our hope was restored, and we could see what we had been longing for, disappointment hit once again. We finally surrendered and could see the Gate, but we could not go through. And, it is our fault. We have too much "stuff". We want to crawl back into our shell because we feel like we have fallen short of His expectations and standards. The enemy says, "You are not enough, and you never will be enough." But, because we have surrendered to Christ, our thinking has begun to change, and we do not believe that liar as easily any more. We have started to believe the Bible when it says,

"For all have sinned and fallen short of the glory of God."

Romans 3:23

This verse is a beautiful piece of revelation. Of course we cannot fit through the Gate on our own! That is not the way He designed it. Our inability to fit through the Gate has nothing to do with us. It has everything to do with His design. He wants us to need Him. Needing Him is nothing to be ashamed of! Needing Him is a priceless gift! It is in our place of need that we can change. We have to change if we are going to walk on the Narrow Road.

Sometimes we do not realize how much baggage we have until we are standing at the Gate and Jesus is asking us to leave it behind. Right now, He is asking some of you to leave behind bags that you have carried for years. Some of you may be known by the bags you carry. But it is time…time to lay it all down. I am asking the Lord to show you, right now, the things in your life that you have been carrying for too long. Maybe you have been carrying that bag(or bags) for years, or maybe you have only been carrying it for a few weeks. You may have a bag that has been hidden under so many other bags that you forgot it was even there. It is time to let go of that one too. Either way, it is not worth carrying any longer. Take the time right now and pray.

"When He found one of great value, He went away and

sold everything He had and bought it." Matthew 13:46

You are one of great value. He dropped everything...gave up everything...for you. I remember a specific moment in my life when I experienced a greater revelation of His love for me and what He did on the cross. I was undone. I felt unworthy for God to give up His only Child for me.

If you have a child, could you imagine sending him to his death? Now, try to think of one person that could be helped by that decision. Did helping that person make the death of your child worth it? I don't know about you, but I cannot honestly think of one person that could justify that choice. But, that is what God did. Or should I say, that is what Dad did. He thought of me when the Holy Spirit impregnated Mary with His Son - He thought of you. And if only for you, He would have made the same decision. What love...what amazing, beautiful, pure love. We are that special to our Dad. He was not willing to go through the rest of eternity without providing a way for us live with Him. He provided the cross. We get to have an eternal relationship with Jesus because of His sacrifice. Even when those in this world look down on us and call us a nobody, we know we are His sons and daughters. We were born into this world, but our first real breath of life was when we said yes to Him.

"...You are not of the world, but I chose you out of the world..." John 15:19

Our citizenship is not to any country on this earth. We are

citizens of Zion. Claim your destiny that is in His kingdom. He delights when His children choose Him over everything else. He gave up so much in order to give us the option of choosing Him. Knowing that we could say no, He gave up everything anyway.

Why should He expect anything less from us?! To pass through the Gate, to have Him, we must give up everything. Isn't it worth it? We are so close to the Narrow Road. We can see the Gate. We have to choose Him above all of our hurts, pains, regrets, failures, bitterness, loneliness, and depression. It is not just the bad that we hold. Sometimes the things that we hold even more tightly are the good things. Maybe our bags are success, money, careers, popularity, family, or ministries. The Lord is not just asking us to lay our bags of issues down…He is also asking us to lay our bags of success down. I am not sure which bags are more difficult to release.

Many times we begin to draw identity from our baggage, and we would not know who we are without it. We feel like it is just too hard to let go…it is too hard to be obedient. But, we also know we will be left outside of the Gate if we do not change. Hasn't it been long enough? Let us not spend any more time living outside the best He has for us. Take a few moments and ponder. Think of old bags, and think of new ones. What is the Lord saying to you? He is calling your name and saying, "It is your time to be free! It is your time to breathe again!" It is time to leave your baggage behind. The only identity you need is the one He is going to give you.

CHAPTER 3: LETTING GO

During my late teenage years and early twenties, I struggled with self-worth and identity. Though I lived a life doing good things and was "happy," my soul was always restless within me. I did not feel like I knew my purpose. I remember trying to determine what I wanted to study in college. Maybe I would be a Veterinarian - yes, I love animals! Maybe I would do theater - I love the arts! Maybe I would be a judge - I could help so many people! Maybe I would be a musician and concert conductor - I would be great at that too! I could see myself being passionate about anything that came to my mind. I was trying to figure out my giftings on my own. I had no idea what the Lord actually wanted me to do.

My college years were a disaster! I was sick all the time and ended up having to withdraw. Honestly, I think when the heart feels sick, the body falls ill as well. I was an unhappy girl! Even as the years passed and I married my best friend, I continued to struggle with my identity. Not knowing what else to do, I ended up working in the office at the church where my Dad pastors, and started teaching a few dance classes. My sister Kara and I have taken dance since we were young. In the summer of 2011, we asked the Lord if we were to open a dance studio in the community. We began to pray, and the doors flew open! Within six months, we had remodeled our facility and classes had begun. Every day, I felt a little less restless…I felt a little less heavy. Weeks would go by, and I would not even recognize myself. I truly believe that when we begin walking in our destiny and identity, our spirit man settles. I could breathe.

Six months after the studio opened, I was able to leave my job at the church and work full time at our studio. Interestingly, if you had asked me during my teen and young adult years, I would have never said my life would look the way it does. I never dreamed my full-time job would be the director and instructor at a dance studio. I would have never said my calling would have anything to do with dance. I actually had pulled away from dance growing up. I hated it. I did not want to express myself to the Lord that way. But His word says,

"Praise His name with dancing…" Psalms 149:3

I was just unable to recognize that attack on my life when I was younger. I am so thankful for the process He took me through! After Kara and I opened the studio, we began to dream big. We hoped to one day have a dance company. I remember thinking it would be five to eight years before we would have a one. It was just one year after we opened that the Lord so loudly and clearly said to establish the company. With much prayer, we took the steps needed and launched Zion Dance Company.

I was one terrified, insecure dancer that was supposed to help lead this group along with my sister. Wow, what a journey! During the company's first summer, we were invited to a conference in South Africa. We would be ministering our performances as well as teaching workshops. Little did I know what waited for me on that trip.

We were halfway through the week, and it was our evening to minister. There were a thousand people watching and from the first sixty seconds to the last, it ranked up there as one of the worst nights of my life. From mistakes I made in choreography, to my costume messing up during my solo, I felt like the worst dancer out there. I felt like a failure. I remember running offstage during one of the dances, crying, and saying to my husband, "I'm the worst one out there. I'm holding them back." He did not have time to say much since I had to run back on for my next part. I let the enemy have his way with my thoughts for over an hour. I was unable to take control of my mind and emotions. The show ended, and I wanted to scream! The service was not over though, so we went out to join everyone as the worship team began to play. The pastor began to pray, and I bowed my head.

I have no idea what was actually said because when I closed my eyes I was in a different place. I began to weep. I cried so hard and for so long that the floor at my feet was soaked. In those moments, the Lord began to show me the journey of my life. Yes, I had stepped into my calling with the studio, and there was a place of peace in that. But, like I have said before, at times He works with me in layers. I was at a new layer of understanding my need for Him. I was bare before Him, asking again, "Who am I?"

I saw a vision of myself walking in a garden. Topiaries were all around. I was standing in front of one that I knew represented me. I took the gardening shears and began to cut on the tree. I was shaping it into what I thought was right. I kept cutting until the tree was distorted and ruined. I had wasted the tree…wasted my life. I remember feeling the Father's touch on my hands as I still held the shears. I knew He wanted me to let go of them, but I hesitated. I was not sure that I could let go of the shears. I had held them for so long. I knew I could not shape the tree myself, but could I trust Him to shape it?

When I finally let go, to my surprise, the Lord laid the shears down and smiled. I had expected Him to save the tree and still make something beautiful out of it. Was He giving up on me? Did He think I was not worth saving? Had I messed up my life so badly that it could not be saved? Then, I heard so sweetly, "I am not going to fix. I am going to plant new." At that moment, I physically felt something break inside me. I felt Him uproot the tree. It was gone…completely gone. In its place, He planted a fresh, perfect, beautiful tree with rich soil and strong roots. I began crying even more. A weight had been lifted. I felt new. Whole. I had carried the weight of false identity for so long, and now I was ready to see myself as He saw me.

I have lived my life differently ever since that day. When things get difficult, I remind myself that the old tree has been pulled out, and a beautiful new one has been planted. I am beautiful in His sight. And, you are the same. No matter what you think you have done to ruin your life and change the shape of who you are, He is ready to restore you to beauty.

Life is a journey. It is a beautiful journey of trust. The real question is…who are we trusting? That experience in South Africa felt real to me. It was as if I could feel the shears in my hand and the fear in my heart of letting go of them. It was a moment of revelation. We are constantly trusting someone. We trust our employer to give us our paycheck every month. We trust the

Letting Go

waitress to bring us our food after we have ordered. We trust that our husband will love us unconditionally. We trust that the other drivers on the road will stay in their lane. We trust that our pastor will teach us correct theology. Or, perhaps we only trust in ourselves. Maybe we think that we know what is best. We are in a constant state of trusting someone.

In my past, I would get caught up in trusting myself. I can tell you that does not end well. Check yourself. I know some of my examples were light-hearted but really think about it. What would happen if you did not get a paycheck from your boss? Would your life be over, or is there Someone greater that you can trust to provide for you? What would you do if your husband hurt you badly? Would your life come to an end, or do you have a greater Lover in whom you can trust? Jesus can be trusted. I will say that again! Jesus can be trusted! He can see you through any storm. From the difficulties that marriage can sometimes bring to a fender bender on the road, He is there. He is trustworthy and faithful.

I had a beautiful experience with the Lord as He showed me what I had done with my life. I had to decide if I was going to surrender and trust Him, or if I was going to continue to hold the shears. Just like we talked about in the last chapter, I had baggage in my life, and I had to let go. I was in my moment of surrender. I could see that precious Gate and feel His presence.

Just getting to the Gate is not enough. We are called to walk the Road. I was desperate and tired of living the same year after year. So, right there, in Johannesburg, South Africa, I surrendered my life in a fresh way to Christ. I let go of the shears. I let go of years and years of baggage so that I might walk through the Gate of His presence. I wanted to walk that beautiful, difficult Road. I had to trust that my Heavenly Dad knew what was best for me. It is because I *trusted* the Holy Spirit at that moment that I was able to surrender. That encounter with Jesus is forever etched in my heart and is a testimony of His goodness to me.

So, I ask you again, what do you need to let go of? Do you trust Him enough to let go of your baggage? What do you need to release so that you can step through the Gate? I am telling you that it is worth it! Maybe you can process on your own, or maybe you need help. Sometimes we need people in our lives to help us through our journey. Whatever your process needs to look like, please be faithful to it. Releasing your baggage is key. For every bag that falls to the ground, stop and replace it with a memorial stone. Keep building, stone by stone, until there in front of the Gate, you have built an altar. Your altar before the Lord symbolizes that you choose Him over everything else. Wet the altar with your tears. This scripture is your promise…

"Those who sow with tears will reap with songs of joy."
Psalms 126:5

Kneel before those stones and see what the Lord might work in your heart. Go back to the altar from time to time and remind yourself of your testimony. Remind yourself of all He has freed you from and the new life you now have. Even though the enemy may tempt you to pick those bags up again, in those moments remember…

"You will overcome by the blood of the Lamb and the word of your testimony…" Revelation 12:11

Letting Go

Hold on to the promises He has made you. Surrender, let go, sow tears, and a song of joy will surely come from your heart once again. You will be changed...and you will pass through the Gate.

CHAPTER 4: I AM CLAY

Wow. Here we are. We feel lighter and more peaceful than ever before because we are not carrying so much baggage. We remember the altar we built at the Gate, and our hearts are overwhelmed with His love for us. Why does He love us so much? Why would He live through the pain of the cross for us? Was it to take our sin? Of course that happens when we come to the cross, but I do not believe Jesus was only thinking about the sin He would take from us when He died. I believe, when He was breathing His last breath, He was thinking about people. He was thinking about the person underneath the sin. That is where the value lies. The value is put on us.

"For the joy set before Him, He endured the cross..."

Hebrews 12:2

We are His joy! Jesus died thinking of the relationships that would be ignited when people receive the gift of the cross. Some of us cannot imagine anyone seeing us as a gift. We struggle with too many issues and wounds for someone to love us like that. Oh, if I could only see you face to face right now! I would look into your eyes and tell you there is One who loves you that deeply. There is One who can see you, and even in all of your mess, does not judge you or forsake you. He adores you! Jesus knows better than anyone that the Bible says,

> *"It is God's kindness that leads us to repentance."*
> *Romans 2:4*

He is not shouting that we have to get our act together, and if we make another mistake, it is out the door for us! NO! He cares for us!

> *"Look at the birds in the sky: They do not sow, or reap, or gather into barns, yet your Heavenly Father feeds them. Aren't you more valuable than they are?" Matthew 6:26*

I think this scripture is posed as a question on purpose. As women, we view many things through a filter which sometimes causes our sight to become tainted. We begin to see life and

The Narrow Road

everyone in it, through bitterness, disappointment, anger, insecurity, arrogance, fear, and so on. Maybe you think it is not so bad if you only have one of these "issues". However, what if these issues were arrows? What if, instead of fifteen arrows, you had only been pierced by one arrow? Would you be okay with that? Your whole body would recognize that something was wrong. One arrow would still bring significant damage or even death. One arrow would still tell your brain that there is pain and hurt. One arrow would cause you to walk carefully so as not to make the pain worse. Even a slight wind blowing would irritate the wound, and if left untreated, infection is the only thing that would grow. Let the Lord pull out the arrow. Let Him heal you from one arrow or twenty arrows. He can do it! You have not been shot so many times that He cannot heal you. He wants to clean you and bandage your wounds. Let Him! How good it is to feel freedom and wholeness!

"It was for freedom that Christ set us free!" Galatians 5:1

He wants us to live in health and see our life and those in it clearly - with no filters. No judgment. Let Him care for you even as He cares for the birds of the air. You are so precious to Him, and He will heal your pain if you give Him the chance. Another translation of Romans 2:4 says,

"Don't you realize that it is God's kindness that is trying to lead you to Him and change the way you think and act?"

Wow. When I read that version it humbled me again. Jesus loves me beyond my sin and draws me to Himself with kindness. What an amazing thought! All He wants to do is change our heart. When Jesus captures our heart, truly captures it, we cannot help but change the way we think and act. Love changes the way we think and act! Repentance is not about going to the altar. It is not about us making a list of all our wrongs and hoping He will forgive us. He already knows everything we have done and everything we have thought. I think true repentance looks soft. It is humble. When our hearts are moldable, we know we have come to sincere repentance. Genuine repentance is changing the way we think and act, and if we are not ready to be reshaped, we are not ready to repent.

> *"As the clay is in the Potter's hand, so are you in my hand." Jeremiah 18:6*

My prayer is that we would live like clay. His hands know how to shape us better than we could ever shape ourselves. I do not want to be anything except clay in my Father's hands. Every morning when I wake up I want to say, "Lord, today I am clay."

I remember a time in my life that my heart was very hard, and I was not interested in being reshaped. One week before my 13th birthday, the Lord told me who I was going to marry. He gave me a very clear dream, and like any good little sister would, I went and told my big sister! I told her mostly because I did not want to tell Mom and Dad yet. By the time we finished talking she was pushing me down the stairs telling me I had to speak to them.

The Narrow Road

I have wonderful parents, four brothers, and one sister. Mom and Dad always taught us that we could hear the voice of the Holy Spirit. We were taught that the God of *EVERYTHING* has a plan for who we are going to be, where we should live, and even what career we are supposed to have. If those things are important to Him then surely He has a plan and is concerned about who we will marry. I mean, come on! Who we marry is a big part of our lives and how it turns out. Why would we think out of everything in our lives that we get to decide about that part?

I believe that just as He created *ONE* Eve for Adam, that He created *ONE* man that is called to be my husband. God did not line up five women before Adam and tell him to pick. No, Jesus knew the exact woman to create that would complete Adam and be everything to him that he needed. Do not hear what I am not saying. I know God's plan for all of us does not look the same. I also know that the story of our lives change. If someone's husband passes away, or for right reasons they need to divorce, do I feel like God will bring another spouse? Yes, if that is His plan. God only knows how the first husband and second can both be His plan. But, His mysteries are not for us to understand. We are to simply walk in His plan.

I am not sharing any of that to place my beliefs on you or cause you to feel judged. The things I share are only shared out of love and a place of vulnerability. I share my view on this matter only so you understand the depth of the story I am about to tell. After I had shared with Mom and Dad that I felt like God said I was going to marry Ben, they said for me to hide it in my heart and not do anything about it. I was young, and they could not confirm what I was hearing. I was a little disappointed that they were not on board with the whole thing, but it did not shake me. I was pretty set that I heard clearly.

Over a year and a half later I found myself sitting in a room with my parents, Ben, and his parents. I believe it was my Dad who said something like, "I think you two have something to share with each other." I think we kind of laughed and felt a bit awkward. We both shared how the Lord spoke to us and that we knew it meant we would be married one day. Both sets of parents confirmed what we felt, and they asked us how we wanted to move forward.

Ben and I wanted to do more than just say we were "dating". In our culture dating does not always mean commitment. We wanted to make a statement that we were committed to marriage because that is what God said to us. We were not going to "try" this for a while and see how it went. We were going to make a vow to each other before the Lord and our families that was as serious as wedding vows. I know it sounds crazy, but I am more thankful than ever for the commitment we made so many years ago.

In December of 2001 we officially became betrothed. We had about six months that were good, and then everything started to change. To this day I cannot put my finger on exactly what happened, but I know I pulled up about 100 filters. I could not see my relationship with Ben clearly. I could not even see him as a person clearly. I became very hard-hearted toward him and was unkind and bitter. When Ben would walk into a room, I would walk out. I tried not to speak to him, sit near him, or look at him. I rejected him completely. I had so much junk in my heart that I could not face it. I could not deal with it.

This season with Ben did not last a few weeks or months…I wish! Our struggle went on for four and a half years. My parents would talk to me and would talk to Ben, but things never changed. I remember one night my Dad asking me if I just needed to end it. I knew the seriousness of that question and did not take it lightly. I had committed myself to Ben. I vowed to marry him one day. It did not matter how bad things were, I never could say I wanted out. I had to believe in my heart that I heard the Lord speak to me

The Narrow Road

when I was thirteen.

One evening Ben and I both were having some talk time with my parents, and Dad told me that the Lord had given him a word. He had one word that summed up what had grown in my heart. Dad said to me that I had let disdain take root in my heart towards Ben. He then read to me the definition. Disdain means "the feeling that someone or something is unworthy of one's consideration or respect; contempt." Wow. That was like a knife in the heart! Truth can hurt, but truth must be spoken. It hit me hard that night that I would choose to have such hatred in my heart. The Word says,

"Don't think of yourself more highly than you ought to think...don't think that you are better than anyone else." Romans 12:3, 12:16

But that is all I did with Ben for so long. Dad sent us both away and said not come back until we had a word from God. He encouraged us to ask the Lord for a fresh word to reconfirm what the He had said to us years ago. I went to my room, got my Bible, and laid in my bed. I was frustrated and confused, angry, and honestly, quite hopeless. I opened my Bible, looked down and read,

"Stop doubting and believe." John 20:27

I fell apart. I wept, alone in my room, and for the first time, recognized that I was miserable enough to let the Lord begin to chisel away the wall I had built. It was time for me to stop fighting and doubting what I knew the Lord had said to me.

Time went by, and I graduated in May of 2005. After graduation, I moved a little over an hour away from my parents to live with my sister and her husband. I felt like I had to get away. I had to pull myself out of the norm and just hide away with God. I spent all summer with Kara and Casey, and most every night the three of us sat together and talked. Well, mostly Casey spoke! I just sat and listened to the wisdom that was shared. I faced what I did not want to…I faced my own sin.

"Why do you see the splinter that's in your brother's or sister's eye, but don't notice the log in your own eye?"

Matthew 7:3

I did not let myself turn the other way, but confronted insecurities and dealt with identity. It was uncomfortable…but discomfort is what my soul needed. I had fed my flesh for far too long and had grown very comfortable in my sin. Ben had his own journey through all of this and had things the Lord worked in his heart, but this book is about my journey. It is not for me to tell what happened with Ben, but for me to tell of my sin, repentance, and redemption. It had become second nature for me to see all the splinters in Ben's eye, never seeing my own log, and judging him harshly for his sins.

"Don't judge…Whatever you deal out will be dealt out to

The Narrow Road

you." Matthew 7:1, 7:2

What a hard lesson...a lesson to love and not judge.

"Imitate God like dearly loved children. Live your life with love..." Ephesians 5:1

Love is the most important. I had to learn to love Jesus more than myself and my "rights". What places in your heart are hard and calloused? Where have you grown disdain instead of love and honor? Where have you thought of yourself better than others? These are not comfortable questions, I know. But, like many of you, I know the brokenness and despair of a life that chooses darkness, not Light. Though the refining process is painful, it is well worth the discomfort to have the reward of walking the Narrow Road.

"He will sit as a refiner...He will purify and refine them like gold and silver. They will belong to the Lord, presenting a righteous offering." Malachi 3:3

As an eighteen-year-old girl, the choice I made to move that summer, to heed counsel, and deal with myself drew me closer and closer to the Road I so desired to walk. Of course then, I did not know that the scripture about the Narrow Road would mean as much to me as it does today. That scripture is like a deep root that has been planted in my heart. But, He knew it. Jesus knew then that my story, which was so difficult to live through, would end up in the pages of this book. What a treasure this testimony is to me.

I encourage you! Do not lose heart! Press on! He knows everything you are walking through. Every disappointment, every hurt, every emotion you have is before Him. He can and He will use it for your good.

"We know that God works all things together for good for the ones who love Him." Romans 8:28

He can do it! Love Him more than you love yourself...more than you love your pain. Let Him work in your heart. When He works, it is supernatural. We will find ourselves receiving peace, love, and courage in moments that we should feel angry and offended. We are to look strange to this world.

"Don't be conformed to the patterns of this world, but be transformed by the renewing of your minds..."
Romans 12:2

The Narrow Road

Yes, Lord! Renew our minds every day! Help us be brave enough to let Your light shine upon our hearts. Speak to us about who we are in You. Open our eyes to see ourselves the way You see us. Let us find our identity in You alone!

Finding true, and full identity in Christ is the key to moving forward. The summer of 2005 was a pivotal season in my heart. I had to make things right between me and the Lord before I could begin to make things right with Ben. As I look back, my heart is full of thankfulness for that summer. I am always grateful for Kara and Casey who played a vital role in that season of refining, and who loved me enough to say hard things.

As the Lord continued to work and shape my heart, I grew soft again. Things were not great with Ben, but we were both trying. We were both seeking the Lord and putting Him first before our relationship. One day the Lord said to me so clearly, "You are missing out on the treasure I have for you." I knew He was speaking about Ben. I knew at that moment, the very person I had viewed as worthless would become the person I would treasure most. I was not sure how that would happen, but I knew that was a promise from my Heavenly Father.

Weeks and months went by, and Ben and I had had several opportunities to minister along side each other and do life together. One of my most precious memories is of Ben's kindness. After all those years of my hardness and hatred towards him, he was always there. He never left. I am not saying it was easy for him because it was not! I remember so clearly the moments when I would think to myself, "I don't deserve this. How can he still love me after all this?"

The Lord did work in my heart and tear down the walls I had built between me and Ben. However, the Lord also used Ben's kindness to soften and crumble those walls as well. It truly is kindness that draws us near. It was hard to not look at myself with guilt and frustration. I also remember thinking, "Stop being kind to me! You are not supposed to treat me this way when I've been so hateful!" When you know that you are guilty, it is hard to receive forgiveness. Isn't that the greatest gift? Where there is true forgiveness, there is love.

That sounds like a man who saw me when I was a sinner, yet still died for me. Even before I asked for forgiveness, He paid the price with hope that I would choose Him. I think somewhere deep inside Ben walked his own Narrow Road. He continually forgave my hatred. He showed love and kindness hoping that I would return and accept him. What a blessing he is in my life. He truly followed Christ's example.

> *"Husbands, love your wives, just as Christ loved the church and gave himself for her." Ephesians 5:25*

I think Ben always looked at me with hope, saw me as his wife, and the Holy Spirit just did His thing. I love that when I see Ben, I see Christ in his eyes. On October 1st, 2006, we got engaged, and on August 10th, 2007, our wedding day, a promise was fulfilled. A vow Ben and I made in 2001 to one day be married became reality, and it was truly a day that the Lord had made.

See, walking the Narrow Road looks many ways. We have many areas in our lives. What does it look like to walk the Narrow Road in each of those areas? As a young woman, one of the ways I walked that Road was by choosing to keep myself pure. I wanted to be able to give myself wholly to one man.

> *"She brings him good and not harm all the days of her life."* Proverbs 31:12

Bringing him good does not start the day you get engaged or get married, and it does not stop on the days he is short with you or hurts you in a deep way. We are to bring good to our husbands *ALL* of our days. I did not date, but I saved myself for the man the Lord had for me. I know that sounds crazy, but that is walking the Narrow Road. That was me choosing to bring him good all the days of my life. Again, I am just being an open book. I am not judging or putting my beliefs on anyone. I hope to encourage and strengthen those who are walking the Narrow Road.

As a teenager betrothed to Ben, it took a lot longer to find the Road. I was conceited and had eyes that could not see. I had a lot of baggage I had to drop. I had many stones to build my altar. What a treasure I received in my life once I let go and let Christ work Himself into who I was. Walking the Narrow Road through betrothal looked like learning to love Jesus more than I loved myself, and dealing with my identity. I was refined and shaped into a beautiful bride. I encourage you to let the Lord form you. Be like clay in His hands. Ask the Lord to show you what it looks like to walk the Narrow Road in your relationships.

CHAPTER 5: THROUGH THE STORM

As I sit down to write, my mind is actually thinking about you. Maybe I know you, maybe I don't, but my heart is drawn to pray for you. So, that is what I have been doing for the last several minutes. My prayer is that you would experience His healing touch in your life and receive every bit of His unfailing love.

"Love never fails." 1 Corinthians 13:8

It does not matter what you are walking through right now; His love for you will *NEVER* fail!

"When you pass through the waters, I will be with you;

The Narrow Road

when through the rivers, they won't sweep over you. When you walk through the fire, you won't be scorched, and flame won't burn you... Because you are precious in my eyes, you are honored, and I love you." Isaiah 43:2 & 4

He. Loves. You. He cares for you. It matters to Him what happens to you. When waters come your way, He does not leave! He walks through them with you. He is your shield from the flames. Christians are not exempt from trials and difficult times! We should be the ones who get attacked the most and, for some strange reason, are peaceful with it.

"If the world hates you, know that it hated me first." John 15:18

Jesus is not asking us to live a life that He was unwilling to live Himself. He lived it. He was a man. He had loved ones and He had enemies. His example to us was to stay steady on the Narrow Road. How do we respond when trouble and heartache come our way?

"We even take pride in our problems, because we know that trouble produces endurance, endurance produces character,

and character produces hope." Romans 5:3-4

Do we look at our problems like that? When issues come up, do we really count it as joy? Sometimes it is one thing after another, and we feel like we cannot get a break. We cannot breathe. In those moments do we count it joy?

For me, I have to be careful to not fall prey to the lies of the enemy when he tells me I am a victim. Being a helpless, hopeless victim does not start when something happens to me or when someone violates me in some way. No, it starts when I let it. It is my choice. It is your choice. It is your "yes". I love you, and I am being real. You are the one who decides to live as a victim or not. Nobody on this planet gave you your identity, so why would you let them take it away? Who you are came straight from Heaven.

"Before I created you in the womb I knew you; before you were born I set you apart." Jeremiah 1:5

That defines "amazing" on a whole new level! Before He even put our bodies together, He knew us! I believe that He has been giving us our identity for more years than we have been breathing. I believe that before we took our first breath He was saying, "I know you." Before we were in our mothers' womb, He was saying, "I love you." That is who we are. We are "the known" of God. We are loved by Him!

Yes, He gave us talents. He calls us to do all kinds of different

The Narrow Road

things, but that is not who we are. Having identity in Christ means two things to me. First, it means that I know what He says about me and believe it. If He calls me His daughter then that is who I am! The second step is to be satisfied with what He says about me. I think the second step is what gets most of us who are struggling.

Knowing that Jesus thinks of us as a daughter is probably not a new concept. We have heard that for years. Being satisfied as a daughter is another whole thing entirely. It sounds terrible that we would not be content being a princess to the King of ALL kings! But, when we let our hearts be shaken, and our eyes wander, that is exactly what we are doing. If our feet stray from the Narrow Road, it is because we are discontent with who we are and what we have. We think there is something better out there, so we choose stuff, other people, hurts, or our rights over Him. Our identity gets wrapped up in our pain or another person, but those things are not who we are. We have to find our peace in being a child of the King. When we settle into our new family, taking our rightful place in His kingdom, there is nothing more fulfilling. You will not need anything else.

I am not talking to you about something that I have not struggled with myself. My life has been a constant journey of choosing to let Him tell me who I am and believing it. Believing what He says can sometimes be the most difficult part. He is trustworthy. Christ's desire for us is to know who we are in Him. His hope is that every day we would push aside the things that the world offers in exchange for our identity. He wants us to live in a constant choice of walking the Narrow Road.

In some seasons this is easier than others, I know. One evening Ben and I were out celebrating our betrothal anniversary. I do not know why but a question popped into my head, and I really wanted to ask him. I do not know why I thought it would be a good moment for it, but, while riding in the car, I spilled out the question, "Have you ever dealt with pornography?" I do not know if I was hoping for trouble or hoping to be proud of the "no" I thought was coming. Ben pulled into a parking space, parked the car, and just looked at me. I knew that was my answer. He began to tell me his story with how it all started, and I grew very angry. I was angry at Ben, I was angry at the person who first showed him pornography, and I was angry at God.

In an instant, I exchanged my identity for the pain Ben offered me. I let it happen. My bitterness and frustration were my own doing because, in that season, I did not know who I was in Christ. I was the victim. Yes, everyone have pity on me! I am the one hurting. I am the one devalued. Ben just needs judgment, right? He needs to know how badly he hurt me. That theory makes a lot of sense to the world but not in the kingdom of God. Behavior in His kingdom looks like this...

> *"Put aside all bitterness, losing your temper, anger, shouting, and slander. Be kind, compassionate, and forgiving to each other, in the same way God forgave you in Christ." Ephesians 4:31*

For this particular situation, I think this scripture sums it up. As women, we like to hold on to bitterness as long as possible, lose our temper, and shout because it is our right! But, those are the exact things that we are to put aside. However, that night in the car I was not interested in putting anything aside.

I do not remember talking about it very much at all after that.

The Narrow Road

It was not until after we were married that the issue was brought up again. I believe it was about a year into our marriage when I came back to Ben and asked if he still dealt with pornography. To my heartache, the answer was yes. Feelings that were not dealt with, combined with new feelings, added up to even more bitterness and a very hard heart.

I remember leaving the room, grabbing my Bible and having a good cry. I stayed alone until I felt like I could make good choices. Before I had left the room, Ben asked me to please forgive him. At that moment, I did not respond. However, I did go back to him and forgive him. The Lord had given me grace and strength through His Word to forgive. Somehow, I kind of had joy in forgiving him…until my own sin was revealed. It was not really forgiveness with the attitude I had on the inside. I went from victim to martyr. It was not enough for him to know how badly he hurt me anymore. He was going to know my pain and have to deal with how "awesome" and "righteous" I was now.

Honestly, I did not deal with anything. I did not let go. I held his pornography issue over him like an umbrella. Little did I know that my actions were keeping him from being washed in the goodness of the Rain. I liked to think that my poor choices only hurt Ben, but that is not how it works. We hurt ourselves most in the process of proving our righteousness. When I held that umbrella over Ben in the spirit, I was holding it over my head as well. Unforgiveness is a trap we set for others that we end up caught in ourselves and left to die alone.

Time went by, and I heard a little voice in my head say to ask Ben how he was doing. It was as if the Lord would always put this little nudge in my spirit right around the time Ben would start struggling again. He would go for long stretches of time doing really well, but it is like I always knew when he messed up. It always took me a little while to work up enough courage to ask him about it. I mean, what woman wants to ask a question to her husband that could cause her pain?

I never could separate Ben's sin from myself. I always felt like it was partially my fault that he still dealt with pornography. I always felt devalued and less than. I felt second best. On occasion, Ben would say he was doing well, but over and over I was met with hurt and tears. Each time I would talk to the Lord, and each time I would "forgive". Time after time, I felt like I had actually given sincere forgiveness. If I had any anger at all, I just called it my righteous anger. The last time I asked Ben how he was doing, I was not even kidding myself anymore. There was not anything righteous about my anger. If he wanted to look at naked girls, then he could go right ahead, but he was not getting me anymore.

Once again, I became very hard and very cold hearted. I could have cared less if he ever looked at me or touched me again. We shared the same house, but we did not share a life together. I was so tired of going through this with him and felt like I had been wounded enough. I had forgiven over and over, and now I was done. I did not forgive when he asked for it, and I did not love unconditionally. I told him that I would stay married to him, but that he did not have my heart anymore. It just was not right! It was not fair! He could not have sin in his life and a happy marriage. He could not have me and all those other girls! He could not have both!

For some of you, you are crying right now because you are walking this same road. Some of you might have tears of joy because you have a testimony from a situation like this. Some of you may be weeping because your story goes beyond pictures into the brokenness of adultery. Others of you are only crying because of your compassion for women who have had to walk this journey. For all of you, I thank God. I thank Him because each of us has a journey to walk and a story to tell. The problem comes when we get stuck in a chapter and decide to live there and read it over and over. I am pleading with you! Please read on! Read further into your story. Let Jesus help you write the next chapter. If your life has been touched by pornography, His touch is greater! He can turn everything for good! That is my testimony, and He wants to do the same for you!

It was in November of 2013 when I found out Ben was struggling again. It was literally the worst Thanksgiving and Christmas in the world! I wish I could paint a vivid enough picture for you. I mean, my heart felt like it did back when we were betrothed. I hated Ben. Hatred felt all too familiar and that scared me. I did not want to go back to the old ways, but I did not feel strong enough not to be overcome by it. I did not want to talk to Ben or look at him. It was awkward to be alone with him, and, honestly, I was happier when he was not around.

Depression consumed me. On a daily basis, I would put the girls down for a nap and find myself weeping. I also found myself looking through a box of special things I kept from our betrothal years. Without realizing what I was doing, I would find myself staring at our betrothal rings for like an hour! Our rings said "true love" on them. I hated that! There was not anything true about our relationship, but day after day the Lord began to speak to me.

It took weeks for me to want to open my ears to hear what the Holy Spirit might be saying. One afternoon I felt like I was supposed to look up some definitions. I looked up what true meant. True means "real, genuine, faithful as to a friend." I did not like what I read at all because the truth began to shine in my life. It hurt so much to let the Lord start the healing process. I knew at that moment the journey was not just about Ben finding freedom. The journey was about both of us finding freedom. For years, I had let my hurt and bitterness define who I was because pornography had touched my life. On my own I chose depression instead of joy. I chose death instead of life. I chose to walk myself right off the Narrow Road leaving my identity behind. I exchanged my daughterhood in Christ for the chance to be a victim. I was not content to be His princess. I had become wrapped up in being Ben's wife instead of Christ's Bride, and when this trial hit, I was not ready.

> *"Therefore, pick up the full armor of God so that you can stand your ground on the evil day and after you have done everything possible to still stand." Ephesians 6:13*

I was not ready because I did not have on my armor. I am not sure why we think we can make it through a war without any armor! It is time to rise up as women of God and fight with righteousness and dignity. When the enemy shows up, it is time he sees a woman in full armor! Let's not be easy prey!

> *"Be strong in the Lord and in the strength of His might." Ephesians 6:10*

One of my favorite prophetic words I have received is the phrase "you are a warrior princess". I want to be a woman full of courage and bravery but also grace and beauty. I pray that same word over you now! Be filled with strength and true righteousness in His power! Be filled with beautiful grace and dignity in the splendor of His royalty. Let's uncover who we are in Him that we may be ready for the testing of our faith.

> *"After all, you know that the testing of your faith produces endurance." James 1:3*

The Lord continued to speak to me and use the symbol of our betrothal rings to soften my heart. Almost daily, I looked at them and wept for the loss of my beautiful marriage. However, it began to hit me that if such a trial was causing so much grief, maybe my marriage was not as healthy as I thought. I am not saying we were not happy because we were. I remember saying to each other multiple times that we felt like we had a Heavenly marriage. Our marriage was a blessing to us, but deep down something was not right.

Ben had his issues he needed to deal with, and I had my insecurities and identity struggles to work through. So, I pose this question…who sinned in the story I told you? Was it just Ben? Did he do all the wrong? He had an identity issue that drove him to an unhealthy place that fed his addiction. Was I not the same? I had an identity issue that drove me to an unhealthy place that fed my addiction. Does it really matter if we are feeding the spirit of lust or the spirit of hate? I fed my insecurities with a fake sense of righteousness…and I am telling you now, that is the spirit of religion, and it has got to go! I fed my hate with the victim mentality saying, "I'm in the 'right' here. How could he do this to me?" I fed and I fed on rotten fruit. Am I no different than Ben? My answer is…no.

It took a long time to come to that revelation. As I began to see a little more clearly, I thought maybe, just maybe, I would want to reconcile with Ben. However, it still took more time. It had never taken me so long to forgive before, but that was the next step. I knew I was going to eventually need to go back to that and not pretend like things did not happen. I had walked in my depression and hate for many weeks by this point. It was not okay for me to ignore Ben's request for forgiveness any longer. I fought with the Lord for days and days about it. When I would think about saying I forgive you, I never could finish that sentence well. My heart would always say, "I forgive you…*BUT* if you fail again I am done loving you." "I forgive you…*BUT* this is the last time I am going through this with you." "I forgive you…*BUT* if you ever do this again I am leaving!" I always had such difficulty leaving off the last condition to my forgiveness.

"As the Lord forgave you, so also forgive each other."

Colossians 3:13

I knew that was the right thing to do. I knew that Jesus had forgiven me so how could I not do the same for the man I loved? I fought with myself saying maybe, because of the number of times he broke my heart, I could get off the hook. Then, in the quiet of my thoughts I heard,

"'Lord, how often will my brother sin against me, and I forgive him? As many as seven times?' Jesus said to him, 'I do not say to you seven times, but seventy times seven.'"

Matthew 18:21-22

So, I asked the Lord, "How many times will Ben sin against me, and I forgive him?" That thought did not seem fair. Jesus being crucified on the cross when no sin ever entered His body was not fair either. He died on that cross for you and me because love never fails! Jesus did not die to show His power or glory. Those things are evident, yes, but He died because He loves us.

There will be moments in our lives that we will have to put aside what is fair to show a Love that never fails. That is what I learned when the Father said to me, "You have to change just one word. You must give forgiveness this way: 'I forgive you...*and*...'" I began to weep and melt to the floor during this moment with my Heavenly Dad. I felt His arms strong around me as His truth settled in me. I was broken. I had no fight left in me. My heart was in so much pain, but I finally longed to be free from myself. I realized that the Lord intended for me to be

"A wife of noble character..." Proverbs 31:10

Not only was I going to forgive, but I was going to forgive this way: "I forgive you...*and* if your eyes wander away from mine I will love you even then." "I forgive you...*and* I will faithfully walk through this with you each time until you find freedom in Christ." "I forgive you...*and* 'you are precious in my eyes, you are honored, and I love you.'" (Isaiah 43:4) That is the truest kind of love.

When we can put our feelings aside and forgive with such

sacrifice, then we have learned what true love is. Let us put away all the bitterness and hurt that the world says we have a right to. Forgiveness with conditions attached is not forgiveness at all. This was the journey the Lord had me on.

After four months, I finally came back to Ben. It was the end of February, and we were going out for Valentine's Day. I wrote him a letter and shared about what God did in my heart. I forgave him that night the way my Heavenly Father taught me. I gave him a necklace as a symbol of my testimony. I put my betrothal ring and a key on the necklace and gave it to him as a gift. I explained my journey through learning what *TRUE* love is. "Faithful as unto a friend." Benjamin Myers has been a friend to me my whole life. He has been my friend through wonderful years and absolutely terrible years, and my desire was to be faithful to him.

I am only responsible for myself. It does not matter what Ben does; it matters that I stay on the Narrow Road. When I stand before my Father, we will not be talking about Ben's journey. Jesus will be looking at my journey, my heart, my feet. Where did I walk? What did I choose? I want to be a daughter that my Dad is proud of. I want to look like Him.

> *"Adopt the attitude that was in Christ Jesus."*
> *Philippians 2:5*

My desire is that I would truly have the character, the attitude, of Christ Jesus living and moving in me. I want to have compassion for my husband when he walks through trials. What if I am part of his journey to healing and freedom? I believe my choice to love is what began to remove the umbrella from Ben's life and from mine. I believe my choice to forgive brought a downpour of His healing rain. We were washed and made clean. Jesus can make you whole again too! Receive His loving, healing rain. There are not many experiences sweeter than being washed by His Spirit when you know you are guilty. It is His gift to us.

> *"Look, I am making all things new!" Revelation 21:5*

We can be a new creation if we will receive the love and the work of the Holy Spirit! "What can wash away my sin? Nothing but the blood of Jesus. What can make me whole again? Nothing but the blood of Jesus." These words move my heart to love Jesus more today than I did yesterday. He never gives up on me! And He will never give up on you! If we humble ourselves at His feet, He will make us new again. I am thankful for my testimony. It was a deep work in my heart, and it has brought about such good fruit.

I see Ben differently. I love him differently. Through our Father's grace, both Ben and I have found freedom. It was not about us trying to change each other and "fix" our problem. It was all about learning who we are in Christ. We let our problems tell us who we are too many times! If we would believe what Jesus said about us, then our circumstances would no longer define us. As I began to live out that revelation, my perspective began to shift.

> *"Her husband entrusts his heart to her, and with her he will have all he needs." Proverbs 31:11*

That is my desire. I want to be the keeper of my husband's heart. I want to be a safe place and a refuge for him. I want to be a support and encouragement. How can I do that the way Christ wants me to if I am letting other things tell me who I am? How can I be a safe place if I am exchanging my identity for fear? How can I love my husband well if I am exchanging my identity for hate? I cannot. It is that simple. If I am not right with God, if my feet are not on the Narrow Road, I cannot be Christ to others.

What is our Father speaking to you right now? Who is He calling you to forgive? "I forgive you *AND*..." What a lesson to be learned! Do not be overwhelmed! The Lord knows what your process needs to be. He knows the pain that you have walked through. Maybe you are walking a path similar to mine. Maybe it is a different situation, but my story is encouraging you to make your own right choices. That is really all I hope. For this entire book, all I hope is that you would be encouraged by my stories to make new decisions. My hope is through my testimonies His Spirit would inspire you to walk every day on the Narrow Road.

CHAPTER 6: A BETTER WAY

Just as Mary poured out everything to show her love for Jesus, I want to do the same with my life.

> *"She began to wet His feet with her tears. She wiped them with her hair, kissed them, and poured the oil on them."*
>
> *Luke 7:38*

Mary not only poured out from her heart, but also from a place of financial sacrifice. She spent it all on Jesus. Her oil was costly but so was the work that Jesus had done in her life. She made an exchange that day. Isn't that what it is all about? It is time to stop making exchanges that benefit us and our selfish ways. Let us be women who make exchanges that further His kingdom in us and on this earth.

Mary was not perfect. Mary was a sinner. She was known by her sinful ways and still the Lord had compassion on her. The heart of the Father was moved by her worship, and her life was changed from that moment. Jesus explained to Simon that he who has been forgiven much will love much.

> *"This is why I tell you that her many sins have been forgiven; so she has shown great love." Luke 7:47*

It is overwhelming to look back at all the wrong we have done and know that His blood has covered it all. The beautiful, rugged cross paid the price for every debt. We have been shown great love through His forgiveness. How can we not show great love in return? It is the exchange. Love for love. Love is the character of Christ. We are to imitate His character as we walk out our lives on the Narrow Road. Having wealth does not keep our feet steady. Driving a fancy car does not lead us to the Narrow Road. Being popular does not have anything to do with walking successfully.

> *"I am the way and the truth and the life. No one can come to the Father except through me." John 14:6*

Jesus is the key! He is the only way! The Narrow Road leads to one place…the Father. We should constantly be traveling towards the Father. If anything leads us away from that destination, then we should know better than to follow it. Hard things have to be said with love so that we can grow in Christ. It is iron sharpening iron.

"As iron sharpens iron, so a friend sharpens a friend."
Proverbs 27:17

I love you so much and want to see Christ be strengthened in you! So, this is what I would say when you are faced with a path that leads to the Father and with one that leads away…if you know better; walk better. When all others around you are pulled to the highway, consumed with their own desires, stay steady! Do not stand on a road where many travel. You know better!

"The truly happy person…doesn't stand on the road with sinners…" Psalms 1:1

"He is your constant source of stability…" Isaiah 33:6

Keep your feet steady and walk the Narrow Road. Walk better! He is your strength and stability. Our path is not just difficult because of the obvious forks in the road but also because of the small ones. An obvious fork in the road could be something like - adultery leads you away from the Father, but faithfulness keeps you steady. Or, stealing leads you off the Road, but honesty keeps you walking forward. I am not saying these are not battles for some. If you have had a root of unfaithfulness or deceit in your heart, I am asking the Holy Spirit to touch you right now! I am praying for complete restoration in your life and that you would begin to exchange those things for a life of freedom!

However, for many of us the fork in the road seems ever so slight. We do not even realize we are fading away from the path. It comes in the moments when we choose to raise our voice in anger towards our children. We fade when we let bitterness grow in our hearts because our husband has treated us unfairly. The fork in the road appears when we decide to use people around us for our gain rather than thinking of them as better than ourselves.

> *"Don't do anything for selfish purposes, but with humility think of others as better than yourselves." Philippians 2:3*

It is the everyday happenings that present us with our choice of walking the Narrow Road or walking away from it. If we know that one road leads to the Father and one away, why would we ever choose to leave Him? So, I will say it again…if we know better; let's walk better.

There was a season in my life that I did not know better. I had just gotten married and was a bit overwhelmed with adjusting to life as MacKenzie Myers. I loved Ben so much, and we had a good marriage. Although, the first five months were a little challenging. I was getting used to all of Ben's habits and trying to figure out how to not judge him because of those habits. Come on now, let's be honest. Wives are almost in a constant state of judging. We are judging what we consider good habits with an eye of approval, and we are judging what we call bad habits with an eye of self-righteousness. We filter everything our husbands do. In our perspective, they are either benefiting us or harming us. At least that is the way we play it. Man, how blind we are to walk this way.

For five months, I watched everything Ben did and felt like I had the scales to weigh his every action. By the end of the year, I was exhausted from feeling so "spiritual" and began to cry out to the Lord for a new way....a better way! The normal way wives looked at their husbands and talked about them did not seem right to me. Something was off. After our first Christmas, I felt like the Lord gave me a strategy for the next year. I was a little overwhelmed by it, but I was desperate enough to try something different.

On January 1st, 2008, I opened a new journal, I opened my Bible, and I prayed that God would show me what to write. I felt like the Holy Spirit asked me to write a scripture in the journal every day. Not just any scripture, but a scripture that was about a "man", a "person". I was to write scriptures that would encourage and strengthen Ben as a man of God. After I had written the scripture in the journal, I was to write a short prayer that went along with it. I felt like the Holy Spirit said to do this every day for an entire year, and then I was supposed to give the journal to Ben as a gift. The Lord was speaking to me about not "speaking". It was time to be quiet, thoughtful, and prayerful. I needed to stop thinking that I was the one who should reward Ben for doing right and judge him when he did wrong. It was not my job to change Ben. I needed to let Jesus do His thing in Ben, and honestly, I needed to let Jesus do His thing in me.

Maybe I did not vent my feelings out loud for the whole world to hear, but poisoning myself happened quietly. As I complained to myself, I began to feel like I was the "better" person. A complaining wife who is constantly trying to fix her husband is a woman shackled to her own insecurities. When we are trying to change something in our spouse, maybe we should first look inward. We should ask ourselves these questions. Why does this really bother me? Is it just a pet peeve? Do you feel alone and devalued, praying that your husband would be the "spiritual" leader you need? From small things to big things, we have to let go of our rights. Remember, we gave up those rights when we said yes to Jesus. However, we still try to weasel them back into our marriage, and we think that is okay. It is not!

You see his socks laying there on the floor(again!) and these thoughts go through your mind, "Why can't he pick up after himself?! Why can't he be a good example for the kids? He sees how hard I work all day, and he still can't help out a little?!" You go to lunch with one of your girlfriends, and she starts telling you all about how her husband prays for her every morning before he leaves for work. She shares about how he is leading their family so well and that he is such a good father. All you are thinking is, "Why can't my husband be more like that? Why can't he step up and be the man our family needs?" All I hear from both of those scenarios is a woman crying out to know who she is in Christ.

It is not about the socks on the floor or the trash bag that has not been taken out. It is not about needing our husbands to step up. These situations just tug on the roots of self-worth and identity that have grown deep in our hearts. We desire to be seen and praised for the work we do in our home and outside of our home. We desire to be valued and cherished by our husbands. We feel like our spouse owes us something. We deal with jealousy when we hear of a marriage that sounds better than ours, but it is because we simply do not know who we are.

We are searching for something from our husbands that they were never meant to give us, and when they fail to deliver, we think we are the victim. Oh, snap! We have got to stop setting our men up to fail! We have got to stop putting them in a place where they do not belong. We can put our men on the throne of our hearts

The Narrow Road

and call it "love", but that is not love. If we loved our husbands, we would seek first the kingdom of God and diligently pursue our relationship with Christ. If we loved our husbands, we would let Jesus tell us who we are. If we loved our husbands, we would desire for them to know who they are in Christ and to be led by the Spirit. Our husbands are our protectors and our lovers, but they should never be our identity. We are only going to know who we are when we know Jesus.

Honestly, I believe marriage issues thrive because the husband and wife do not know who they are in Christ. They do not know how to prefer one another because they do not even prefer Christ above themselves. Jesus is perfect in every way. He gives us the most selfless love of all, and still we do not choose Him every time. If we cannot do that, then how do you think we will ever choose our spouse above ourselves?

I am not saying our husbands should not help out around the house or give us thanks for all we do, but we should not live for their praise. How about when we see the socks on the floor, we serve our husbands and put them away. When their dishes are still on the table, we clean them up. When we see potential in our men, we pray for them to walk in it. We do not preach at them. It is not up to us to change them. Know who you are and serve. Serve your husband as if you were serving the Lord.

"Whatever you do, work at it wholeheartedly as though you were doing it for the Lord and not merely for people."

Colossians 3:23

A Better Way

Serving keeps us on that beautiful Narrow Road.

> *"You should clothe yourselves instead with the beauty that comes from within, the unfading beauty of a gentle and quiet spirit, which is so precious to God." 1 Peter 3:4*

The year of journaling and praying for my husband was about me learning the meaning of a gentle and quiet spirit. Some days it was difficult because I would be frustrated with Ben about something from the day before. I would not want to write a prayer for him! But I did…every day. For one year, I kept my heart in the secret place. I blessed my husband on days that I wanted to and on days that I did not want to. See, it is not about feelings. God did not tell me to write in Ben's journal only on the days that it felt good. If I had done that, there would not have been any growth. No lesson would have been learned. To tell you the truth, that year of journaling ended up being so much more about me and Jesus then it did about Ben. It was about me obeying the Holy Spirit and longing to *KNOW* Jesus even on the days that I did not *FEEL* Him.

I am pretty sure we would all agree that being a drug addict is unhealthy. It is wrong. It is sin. The definition of addicted is "physically and mentally dependent on a particular substance, and unable to stop taking it without incurring adverse effects." The addict is "the person who is addicted to a particular substance". I hear those definitions, and my heart breaks for every person bound by such chains. I was bound. We get caught up in thinking a person addicted to illegal drugs is the main problem. For anyone who has been in bondage to drugs, I do pray that Jesus would make a way

The Narrow Road

for them and pour out His Spirit on them. It is a problem, just not the main problem. We start getting uncomfortable when the Lord shows us our own addictions. Maybe our issue is not drugs. Maybe our addiction is money, clothes, accessories, friends, cars, work, etc.

I believe one of the top addictions that Christians deal with is "feelings". We should be labeled "feeling addicts". Drug addicts are people without identity looking for a fix, and when that wears off they search until they find their next fix. Feeling addicts are people without identity looking for a fix, and when that wears off they search until they find their next fix. That sounds like the same problem to me! That is *NOT* okay!

I am not saying feelings are bad! I am not saying that we do not ever feel Jesus! I have felt Him so many times in different ways, and it is amazing! Being in worship can be a beautiful, emotional experience. The issue comes when we think that is all there is. A follower of Jesus is called to do more than just *feel* God; we are called to *know* Him! If it is all about feelings, we would need our worship team or pastor to make us cry every Sunday. We would need a spiritual conference to get us pumped up. When those things are done, we are lost until the next meeting. It is not about making it from Sunday to Sunday or conference to conference treating them like our "fix". It is about meeting with the Holy Spirit every day of our lives desiring to *KNOW* Him!

The best way to know Christ and know what He says about us is to read His book. It is the best book in the world! It is the only book that is alive! The Word moves and works in our hearts as we read it. Reading the Word is how we get to know Jesus. Reading the Word is how we get Jesus inside of us. The Bible tells us exactly who we are if only we would fully believe what it says.

I learned about Jesus and His character as I faithfully wrote in

Ben's journal. The Father dealt with my heart, and it became a year of difficult, wonderful growth. I had been forgiven so much that it became a blessing for me to show great love in return. By pressing through that year, I not only showed Christ how much I loved Him as I obeyed Him, but I showed great love to my husband. It was a sacrifice to finish that year of journaling, but I learned how to walk better in my marriage.

When I started my marriage I was addicted to my own insecurities and fears. When we walk through life like that it hurts those closest to us. Do not be afraid to go there with Jesus. Soften your heart, and know that His love is unconditional. Ask the Father to show you what things you might be addicted to. What "particular substance" do you crave? Is it the acceptance of others and attention? Maybe your fix looks good on the outside because it is a "spiritual high", but in between Sundays you are miserable and pulled every which way.

"God's goal is for us to become mature adults — to be fully grown, measured by the standard of the fullness of Christ. As a result, we aren't supposed to be infants any longer who can be tossed and blown around by every wind..." Ephesians 4:13-14

Our addictions are close to our heart, so my guess is that you will not have to look far to find them. I know these are not easy things to deal with, but the reward of walking the Narrow Road is far greater than any earthly pleasure we could imagine.

The Narrow Road

Writing in Ben's journal was a strategy God gave me. It helped me walk a path that would take me from being an infant to an adult. Jesus is constantly trying to teach us and show us how to walk as mature adults. It was sneaky of Him because I thought the journal was about Ben when it was really about me! It was a tool the Father used to show me how to walk better.

My marriage is not better because I am a better "wife". My marriage is better because I am a better woman of God. It is all about the choices we make that keep us walking toward the Father. I know I still do it, but my heart aches to never make a choice that would turn me away from Him. I am learning every day what it means to walk the Narrow Road. If who I am as a woman continues to be strengthened in Christ, then who I am as a wife will be wonderful. If I know who I am in Him, then who I am as a mother will be beautiful. If I walk the Narrow Road, then who I am as a daughter and sister will be a blessing. If I remain steady in all circumstances, then who I am as a business owner will be impactful.

See, everything falls into place when we simplify our identity. I do not need the complication of trying to figure out who I am as ten different things! If you noticed, I did not say anything about MacKenzie having to find out who she is as a mother, wife, business owner, etc. I do not need to find out "who I am" as those things. Those things do not define me. We make Christianity too difficult I think. Once our conscience recognizes our sin and we come to the cross, it is as simple as believing that we are sons or daughters of the King. We only need to know who we are as a woman of God! We only need to learn who we are as His daughters to be content in this life. Simplify. That is my advice.

On the 1st of January, 2009, I gave Ben his journal! He now had a prayer and scripture to read every day that was written specifically for him. With Christ by my side, I was able to accomplish what He set out for me to do! Not only was this tool a gift to me, but I had the great joy of sharing it with my mother and sisters. A couple of them felt like the Holy Spirit put it in their hearts to do a journal for their husbands. Even though many of us can use the same tool, all of our journeys will look differently. As some of my family went through their year of writing, it was beautiful to see how the Father worked in their hearts so lovingly.

From my sister-in-law, "Writing the journal for my future husband created a unique and deep connection with my husband's heart and more importantly, the Lord's, in a way I had never felt before. Among my siblings, I was the first and only daughter; so, I encountered little opposition in receiving the love and attention that filled my heart so uniquely. As I began this journal, the Lord used the process as a tool to reveal the necessity of a vital shift from focusing on receiving attention to learning how to prioritize and honor my future husband by putting him before myself."

From my friend Bethany, "Little did I know that the year I committed to journal 365 days of Scriptures and prayers for my husband would be one of the hardest years of our married lives. We received devastating news regarding my husband's career, and I gave birth to a colicky baby who had horrible reflux and never ate or slept until she was five months old. I also had twins that were three months shy of their second birthday when the baby was born. I was exhausted and worn out on all fronts. If it were not for journaling for my husband, I am not sure I would have been praying for him or digging into God's word very much at all that year. Of course, he needed my prayers more than ever, and they helped to transform my own needy heart. God's word always comes more alive to me when I write it down. It is living and active and will change us, even if our circumstances don't change right away."

Ask the Lord for a creative way to walk through your circumstances and how to deal with your addictions. Whatever you are struggling with right now, I know that your Heavenly Dad has a strategy that will benefit you as well as those around you. As a woman of God…

"Don't provide an opportunity for the devil."
Ephesians 4:27

Let's not allow the enemy to have his way in our hearts and homes any longer. Let's stand our ground! We need to strengthen ourselves every day!

"Be transformed by the renewing of your minds so that you can figure out what God's will is — what is good and pleasing and mature." Romans 12:2

My prayer for you is that you would truly know what God's will is for your life and that you would have the courage to obey the Holy Spirit when He speaks to you. If you will soften your heart and listen to His voice, His faithfulness will show you the way to the Narrow Road.

CHAPTER 7: THE MILE-HIGH PILE

As I reflect on the stories I have shared with you, and the lessons I have learned, I hope that your spirit has been able to drink of His fresh water. Today, right where you are, drink of His living water. I know there are times in our lives when things get so busy that we become fragile. We are so weary that when we come to Jesus we do not fully trust that He can revive us. We are like the Samaritan woman at the well. When Jesus tells her of the living water that she should ask Him for, she does not see how it is possible.

"Sir, you don't have a bucket and the well is deep. Where would you get this living water?" John 4:11

When we are weary or hurting, our situations begin to tell us

The Narrow Road

that Jesus does not have the resources to fulfill His promises. To the woman at the well, He promised living water, but how was He going to deliver? She did not see a way. Are there situations in your life that you cannot see a way? Are you fearful because you do not see how the Lord is going to work on your behalf? I have been there. I know others have too, and definitely the Samaritan woman can identify.

> *"Jesus answered, 'Everyone who drinks this water will be thirsty again, but whoever drinks from the water that I give will never be thirsty again. The water that I give will become in those who drink it a spring of water that bubbles up into eternal life.'" John 4:13-14*

The woman asked to be given this living water, but Jesus asked her to bring out her husband first. At that moment, her history was brought to light. She had five previous husbands, and the man she was with now was not her husband. Jesus wanted to make an exchange. It is what we have been talking about through this entire book. Jesus wants us to exchange our sins, regrets, and pains for a life in Him. The Samaritan woman received her living water after making the exchange of her past. Most of us have some regret in our past that keeps us from receiving His living water. Regrets hold us to our past, and our past keeps us at a distance from the Narrow Road. Why would we choose that?

When I was pregnant with my first daughter, I began an interesting journey with the Lord. Just a few weeks into the pregnancy, I started having terrible morning sickness. I was sick all day every day throwing up until I was given some amazing medicine! I had to take the medicine several times a day so that it would not leave my system, or I would start throwing up again. I had heard that once you begin your second trimester a lot of the morning sickness would go away. Being the hopeful person that I was, on the morning I welcomed the second trimester into my life, I decided not to take my medicine! That also happened to be the day that my husband had to stay home with me because I started throwing up every thirty minutes. I had thrown up fifteen times before the medicine started working again. I know this is gross, but I am trying to give you a good picture of the reality of my life during that time! I never came off my medicine after that point. I had to take it all the time if I was going to function and have a life.

Nothing else happened until week 34 when I started noticing some bumps on my skin. Casey, my sister's husband, is a doctor, so I showed him to see if he had any thoughts. After he had done some researching, he thought it was possibly something called "PUPPS" and suggested I go see my obstetrician. Sure enough, Casey was right, and I had PUPPS(Pruritic Urticarial Papules and Plaques). It was just a few spots at first, but in one week's time it was everywhere! PUPPS is a rash that 1% of women get during their first pregnancy. It can spread everywhere except for the face. I had it from my neck all the way to my feet. By 36 weeks, I could not get any relief from the itching and burning. It made me want to tear my skin off!

At my 36th-week appointment, my doctor said we were going to induce. He had literally seen women go crazy because of this rash, and the only way to get rid of it was to deliver the baby. So, we set to induce at week 38! Yay, me! I had two more weeks to go of excruciating pain and no sleep! But, sure enough, at 5:00am on September 24th, 2009, we headed to the hospital! I was super nervous. Obviously, I had never had a baby before, and I was

The Narrow Road

praying for a good experience. I do *NOT* like needles! I was pretty much a zombie because of the lack of sleep, but I tried to enjoy the day as much as possible. At 2:01pm our sweet Hannah-Brooke took her first breath, and they laid her on my chest. There I was. A mother. I had a child. My arms were holding her, and my eyes were studying her. All I could say was, "Man, she looks just like Ben." From there the nurses cleaned her up, and I started trying to breastfeed her…which was simply a disaster. However, we continued with it. On top of that, the doctor told me that my rash would now get worse before it would get better. Again, yay, me!

After many days in the hospital, we went home but that would not last for long. Once Ben headed back to work, we moved in with my parents. I could not be left alone with Hannah-Brooke. My rash progressively got worse for two solid weeks after delivering. It took two more full weeks after that to clear up. During the two weeks that my PUPPS was clearing, I got mastitis. Mastitis overlapped with the flu for two weeks, and I was going insane. I had six weeks of nothing but struggles. My sickness not only affected my body…it affected my soul.

My husband did the best job that he knew how, and my Mom and Dad cared for me pretty much around the clock. I was well loved, but I did not give love well…especially to my new, precious, baby girl. I never held her except when I had to feed her. I never talked to her or loved on her. Ben and my parents changed every diaper for the first three months. They truly cared for her. After a month at my parents' house, we decided to stop nursing. For us, it was just a wise decision if I was going to start fostering any relationship with my daughter.

Once I was healthy enough, we moved back home, and I did start to enjoy my daughter and love on her. I remember one day I sitting on my couch with Hannah-Brook in my lap. No one was around. I looked down at my daughter, and I started to cry. Tears were pouring down my face. At that moment, I realized that I had never said, "I love you," to Hannah-Brooke. She was three months old and had never heard her mother's voice say I love you. Right then and there, I picked her up from my lap, brought her little face right in front of mine, and I said out loud, "I love you...I love you, Hannah-Brooke...I love you." Over and over. I had a place in my heart that needed to confess my love for my daughter. After I was able to pull myself together, I called Ben to share with him what had happened. It was a really special day.

With my second pregnancy, I was sick, but I knew exactly what to take for it, so that was no big deal. However, things got much worse around 15-16 weeks. I thought I was just dealing with a bad stomach bug, but my mom felt like we needed to get it checked out since the pain was so severe. She plopped me in the car, and we were off! They diagnosed me with round ligament pain. It was supposed to be nothing. They said most ladies only deal with it during their second trimester. They also assured me that I had nothing to worry about because so few women have long term problems with this kind of pain. But, after another week of constant pain, we had to move back in with my parents. Ben had taken days off from work to help with Hannah-Brooke, but that could not last forever.

From week 16 on, my pain never left, and it was very severe. I stayed in a bed or on a couch all day. I could not take care of my 1-year-old at all. I could not dress her, bathe her, fix her food, or play with her. We were very thankful for family during that season. My pain was so bad that I would stay awake most nights curled up in a ball crying. For weeks, my parents adjusted their schedules so that they could be home with me. They moved their meetings to their house, and if one had to leave the other would stay home. After a couple of months, others in my family began to help out. My younger brother moved back home from college to help me and care for Hannah-Brooke. Several friends pitched in when my family

The Narrow Road

had things they could not miss.

It was an interesting time. We lived with my parents for about five and a half months. A few weeks before Judah-Grace was born we felt like we had to make the adjustment back home. We needed to give Hannah-Brooke the chance to readjust to living at her house again. Also, we wanted to get the new nursery done. We induced with Judah-Grace at week 38 as well, and as soon as she was born my pain was gone. It was a long journey, but the reward was worth it.

Because of my experience with Hannah-Brooke we did not even try to nurse with Judah-Grace. All I wanted to do was hold her, and love her. She slept with me in the hospital bed, and I enjoyed every moment. I missed out on so much with Hannah-Brooke that I did not want to have the same regrets with Judah-Grace.

But, it is never ok to let regret control your life, and, unfortunately, I did that. I held so much over my head from what I went through with Hannah. When Judah came along I tried to make up for my mistakes. I did not see myself the way Jesus saw me. It took years for me to acknowledge the issues that I held in my heart and to let the Lord restore me. I had regret after regret and saw myself as a failure.

The night before Hannah-Brooke's fifth birthday, Ben and I were putting her to bed and decided to tell her the story of the day she was born. We laid there together, and H listened with a smile on her face. Ben had just gotten to the part where I said, "Man, she looks just like Ben." He meant it well, and Hannah-Brooke liked it! It was precious until I could not keep my tears in any longer, and I had to leave the room. It was like this wave of grief crashed over me.

The Mile-High Pile

My heart and emotions felt like I had just gone through all that pain and sickness again. It felt so real. I had so much regret weighing on me that I was about to erupt. Once Ben finished sharing with HB, he came into our room and sat quietly beside me. I finally stopped crying enough so that I could speak. I told him that it was not his fault, but what he said uncovered some painful memories. It brought up an insecure place in my heart. That night I realized the burden I still carried from both of my pregnancies. I said to him, "I didn't just say she looked like you because she did. I said that because I didn't have anything else to say." I remember that moment in the hospital room all too well. I had no words. I had no motherly emotion. I was ashamed. I did not even think to say, "I love you," to Hannah-Brooke. What a failure as a mom. What a loser to treat a child like that. My child! How could I treat her that way?! How could I not hold her and love her the first three months of her life?! What if I have scarred her? Thought after thought kept pouring out. I had to deal with five years of hidden regret and pain.

A lot of the thoughts seemed too difficult for me to process. The longer I let them grow in my heart, the more I believed what they said. In the deepest part of me, I believed that I was not a good mother. For five years, I listened to that lie. Not only did it affect my relationship with Hannah-Brooke but it also affected my relationship with Judah-Grace. My dolls are amazing, and they have loved me from day one. My regrets made it harder for me to receive their love because I would think, "Well, they don't know how I was when they were born. If they knew how I treated them, they wouldn't forgive me. I wonder how many years I have before they will find out?"

That night before H's birthday, the Lord brought all of this back to my attention. I finally surrendered the issue to the Lord and told Him I wanted to deal with it once and for all. I did not

The Narrow Road

need this wall in my heart anymore.

We grow very comfortable with our walls dividing us from the fullness of who God wants us to be. But why? That is what I asked myself. And you know what? I had no good reason. There was no good reason for me to stay behind my comfortable wall. So, enough was enough. No matter how difficult it was going to be to release and confess what I needed to, I was going to do it!

I felt like the first thing I needed to let go of was the regret I felt as a mother. The second, I needed to stop carrying the burden of all the pain I went through. I can bring back every traumatic emotion when I start to remember the agony of my rash, the round ligament pain, the morning sickness, mastitis, and so on. If I give myself to my memories, I can put myself in a place of panic and fear. That is not where a woman of God is supposed to walk. To be quite honest, back then, I do not know if I knew how to walk better during those times. But, I can tell you one thing. If I had a physical experience like that again, you would not find my soul wasting away with discouragement.

All the days that I laid on a couch or in a bed I never once asked Jesus if there was something He wanted to teach me. Not once. Man, how that grieves my heart today. Even if my body could not have been up and active, my spirit could have been walking the Narrow Road. I was in the perfect condition(twice!) to surrender myself completely and ask God what He wanted to do during that time. I know a lot of days I was extremely sick, and I could not even think straight. A lot of people would just say, "Oh, don't beat yourself up about that. You were going through a really difficult time." I may have been, but Jesus could have made it a little less difficult if I had invited Him into my situation like I know to do today.

Do not let people make excuses for you. Slap it down and run with a passion for the Narrow Road! When it is you standing before Jesus, His ears will not hear the excuses others have made for you. That is a one-on-one date with your Heavenly Father, and He simply wants to know where your feet traveled while you were here on the earth. So, invite Him in. Invite Him into every circumstance that you are going through and watch how faithful He will be!

I know it can be difficult to get time by yourself, but I encourage you to try. When it is quiet, close your eyes and begin to ask the Lord to show you the places where you have hidden your fear, regret, and pain. Begin to write those things down. Let the Lord expand your perspective and bring you healing. Maybe you will want to throw the piece of paper away? Maybe you will want to burn it? Maybe you will want to frame it as a symbol of freedom? In my opinion, the first step to victory is forgiving yourself. That was a big thing for me. I held myself to such a high standard, and if I could not forgive myself then neither could anyone else...or God for that matter!

However, the "high standard" we use on ourselves does not always match His standard. We need to check how we measure ourselves. We all need to do this! We need to stop striving to live up to our standards, so that we can thrive as we live by His standards. *READ YOUR BIBLE*! I know that seems like silly, first grade advice, but most adults are struggling because they do not know what Jesus says about them or what His standards are.

I am thankful it is so simple! I am so grateful that Jesus did not leave us hanging out down here with nothing to help us. Jesus gave us every parable we needed in order to know how to make it through this life. He gave us every love-thought that we needed to hear. He gave us every teaching we needed to learn from so we could live by His standards. Jesus gave us everything we need to know in the Bible!

The Narrow Road

If you are broken, read the Bible! If you are lonely, read the Bible! If you struggle with depression, read the Bible! If you have a temper, read the Bible! If you are struggling with addictions, read the Bible! If you are the victim of some wrongdoing, read the Bible! I am so happy to tell you that I have good news...I have all the answers you need! They are in the Bible! I love His Word more today than I ever have in my entire life! It is breathing inside of me. It is constantly changing me.

I hope you hear my heart and my passion for His Word. We cannot make it in this life without becoming friends with who He is as the Word! It is so important! The Word is a bridge to knowing Christ. I hope you and I both desire to be on that bridge every day of our lives. The other good news I have is this...if you are dealing with any of those issues I mentioned (brokenness, loneliness, depression, anger, etc.), I know the solution for all of them. Know. Who. You. Are. I am going to use my "simple" world again. It is not as complicated as you think, and you are never so far gone that you cannot come back to Him.

See, the enemy likes to pile all these "labels" on us. He wants us to feel like we are way down deep with a mile-high pile on top of us. If satan can convince us that we are buried like that, then he knows we will get discouraged. We start telling ourselves that even if we dealt with one issue every day we would still never be free. When we are convinced of that lie, we quit trying to get free altogether, and satan has won.

Picture the game Jenga. All the blocks stacked up represent all of our issues. If we decide that we can never remove the blocks and be free, then we just get comfortable with them burying us. But Jesus does not play games with our hearts! He wants us to learn and grow. He wants us to become more like Him. He does not toy with us.

The Mile-High Pile

I have been awakened to the fact that without revelation we work the Jenga blocks from top to bottom. We think that because we have gotten ourselves into this mess of issues that we have to dig ourselves out one block at a time. Jesus does not work like that! Jesus works in the business of grace! He comes in, if you will let Him, and finds that one block on the bottom, pulls it, and everything else crumbles. It has to! Written on that one block is the word "identity".

Do not feel like you have to start at the top and work your way through every block. Do not think, "I'll work on my anger first, then I'll move on to my depression, and after that I'll deal with my hurt." First of all, if you want to be truly free, you cannot be the one to pull the blocks out. Jesus is your Savior, and He is the official Block Puller. Second, freedom in this life…from everything…comes when you simply know who you are. You become free from addictions because you find that you do not have a craving for anything less than Jesus. You become free from anger, bitterness, and rejection because you are not holding on to those things as a definition of who you are. If you will get into your Bible, you will find that it says you have been made new!

"This means that anyone who belongs to Christ has become a new person. The old life is gone; a new life has begun!"

2 Corinthians 5:17

I belong to Christ! That is who I am. You belong to Christ! The only Jenga block that needs to be pulled is the one labeled "identity". Don't you think that if you truly believed, like way down deep believed, you belonged to your Heavenly Daddy that all the other blocks would crumble too? They would! Your Daddy would start speaking to you about what He did for you and how He gave everything to have you in His family! He would tell you who you are in His eyes and how much He loves you! This revelation will change your life! I encourage you….*STOP* being distracted by the pile! That is what the enemy wants! He wants you to be distracted and lose your way. He wants you to think that you will never get free. Fight back! Allow Jesus to come in. Let Him pull that block from the bottom. Let's deal with the root issue of it all — identity. We do not need to play games. We do not need to spend years of our lives pulling different blocks out. When Jesus pulls the right block, your mile-high pile shatters.

For some reason, the Lord likes to work on that "identity block" with me when I am acting. Some of my most precious moments with Jesus have been on the Legacy Theatre stage. Legacy is a community theatre in my hometown, and I have had the great pleasure of playing many different roles in their productions. Each part I have played has been unique and deeply meaningful to me. Each role has taught me something about my own identity in Jesus.

I remember playing the White Witch, in the production *Narnia: The Lion, The Witch, and The Wardrobe*, and understanding a greater depth of His love. There is a scene where I stood above Aslan, the lion who represented Christ, and began to mock Him. I tortured Him, and He just laid there. At the end of the scene, I quickly killed Aslan with my sword and left with my army. Once off stage, there was a scene of mourning by Aslan's followers. During this time, there was always this specific chair backstage against the wall that I would sit in and let myself cry. I would listen to the song being played and let it minister to me.

I killed Him. I denied who He was and chose a different path. His blood was on my hands, but when I receive His gift, it is His blood that washes me completely. It was always such a somber and quiet moment. At every performance I was faced with the reality of my sin and the gift of redemption. It was a sweet time of growing closer to Christ, thanking Him for what He did for me. I always felt washed and made whole because of His beautiful sacrifice.

Loreen March is a woman dear to my heart. I played this character in a production called *In His Steps*, and my life was totally changed by the end of it. The story is about a pastor coming to the revelation of what it means to be a Christian and urging His congregation to ask this question in all they do, "What would Jesus do?" It is a powerful production! Loreen March was a former prostitute who comes to know Jesus. In my words, she began walking the Narrow Road. She receives a Bible during one of the scenes and it becomes her greatest possession. Loreen believes everything the Bible says about her. She is not weighed down by the burdens and sin of her past, and she is not caught up in anxiety or fear about her future.

I want you to picture yourself in your sin. Every terrible, awful thing you have ever done. Be honest with yourself, and do not hold back. You need to recognize that you have been caught in the action of committing every one of those sins. Now, listen to this story.

"The legal experts and Pharisees brought a woman caught in adultery. Placing her in the center of the group, they said to Jesus, 'Teacher, this woman was caught in the act of committing adultery. In the Law, Moses commanded us to

stone women like this. 'What do you say?' They said this to test him because they wanted a reaction to bring an accusation against Him. Jesus bent down and wrote on the ground with His finger. They continued to question Him, so He stood up and replied, 'Whoever hasn't sinned should throw the first stone.' Bending down again, He wrote on the ground. Those who heard Him went away, one by one, beginning with the elders. Finally, only Jesus and the woman were left in the middle of the crowd. Jesus stood up and said to her, 'Woman, where are they? Is there no one to condemn you?' She said, 'No one, sir.' Jesus said, 'Neither do I condemn you. Go and sin no more.'"

John 4:3-11

All others have left and it is just you and Jesus. There are always going to be accusers in your life who are ready to throw you into the middle of the group, but they do not define your future. Maybe you were caught in sin, but that is not the end of your story. In the scripture we just read I hear Jesus saying to us all, "I love you. I do not condemn you. Now, go…walk better." It is a gift! His love and forgiveness is a gift! Loreen March did not deserve that gift, but it was given because of grace. As Loreen, I read that John

4 passage during one of the scenes. In those moments, it was like I honestly did not care what anyone else thought of me or how they judged me. I knew Jesus loved me and had washed me clean from all my wrongs. Loreen taught me that if my Heavenly Father does not condemn me then I am not condemned. I would never want to raise an earthly voice above my Daddy God's voice and He says, "Neither do I condemn you. Go and sin no more." Rejoice in that!

If you still feel shame because of what you have done, it is because you feel unworthy. And guess what?! You are not worthy. You don't deserve it and neither do I! That thought needs to become a revelation that empowers us, not one that weighs us down and keeps us from accepting the greatest gift ever! If we deserved what Jesus did for us, then His sacrifice would not have meant much. What a great love Jesus has shown us!

Junie B. also had a lesson about sacrifice and love to teach me. Legacy Theatre did a production called *Junie B. Jones in Jingle Bells, Batman Smell.* I was cast to play Junie B. After the first read through, I was sure that Jesus had a little somethin', somethin' up His sleeve that He wanted to teach me. I never knew a first grader could teach me so much. In the play, Junie B. has an enemy named May. They hate each other! Not only does Junie B. hate May but things get worse when she draws May's name for the secret Santa party. Junie B. tries to puzzle piece a plan together that lets her get the toy she wants from the Christmas shop and still have enough money to buy gifts for her family. She decides the best plan is to not spend any money on May and to give her coal as her secret Santa gift.

I know as adults we do not go around leaving coal on people's desks or in their cars or homes. That is just not nice, and we would never do that to be hateful, right? Sadly, even as adults I am afraid we do leave coal for one another. I was really challenged to be aware of the times that I leave my invisible coal for other people. Being invisible does not mean it is not there. The decision to leave coal for someone hurts me and the person I left it for. Sometimes we do not simply leave the coal for the person that has hurt us, we throw it at them! We pull that coal out from our heart and we just let them have it! I mean, why not? They are the enemy, right? But Junie B. learned a valuable lesson about the exchange Jesus wants us to make. Or should I say I learned the lesson. In the practical, Junie B. did exchange the coal for a real gift for May. It was a very difficult decision, and at the time she made the exchange she was not super happy about it. On the inside, Junie B. began to learn how to exchange her hate for love. What a lesson for a little girl to teach me.

What I was going through in my personal life while working on this production was in a lot of ways what Junie B. had to go through. The blessing Junie B. received in the end was how good she felt on the inside. I want to be like that. It does not matter what situations are going on in my life or what things have happened to me. I want to make the Narrow Road choices that seem impossible to make…choices that shock the world and leave me, as it did Junie B., wondering, "How come I feel so good inside?"

CHAPTER 8: KEYS

See, it is about walking the Narrow Road every moment of every day. It is not about all the different teams you are serving on at your church. If God has called you to serve in your church, then that is wonderful! But, the real journey is finding the Road as you are parenting, when someone offends you, and when you are working through things with your spouse. You have to keep walking the Road when you are at work, and when you feel lost. How do we represent Christ to the world? His Name is either promoted or distorted to those around us by the way we act. Do we represent Him well? Do people see love in us? Do they see compassion?

"Love is patient, love is kind, it isn't jealous, it doesn't brag, it isn't arrogant, it isn't rude, it doesn't seek its own

The Narrow Road

> *advantage, it isn't irritable, it doesn't keep a record of complaints, it isn't happy with injustice, but it is happy with the truth... Now faith, hope, and love remain - these three things - and the greatest of these is love."*
> 1 Corinthians 13:4-7, 13:13

If you are like me, you read that list and think how could I ever live up to all that?? It's too hard! We read 1st Corinthians 13 and think if we live our lives like that we have found perfection. Then perfection becomes our motivation, and we become overwhelmed and insecure because we fall short of perfection on a daily basis…sometimes an hourly basis! It is not our job to be perfect! That scripture is not about us living our lives perfectly with our family and friends. It isn't even in our own power that we could begin to live a true life of love.

> *"With man this is impossible, but with God all things are possible."* Matthew 19:26

When Christ lives within us, love becomes possible. It goes back to the first chapter when we talked about full surrender. If we can begin to put all these things together the Lord is teaching us, then we can start to mature in His ways. His desire is for us to grow up in His kingdom. He does not want us to stay like children.

"When I was a child, I used to speak like a child, reason like a child, think like a child. But now that I have become a man, I've put an end to childish things."

1 Corinthians 13:11

Our Heavenly Father wants us to constantly mature in Him. He wants us to speak, reason, and think like a grown son or daughter of the King. He wants us to represent Him and His kingdom well. We are the ones that the world sees until He returns. What an awesome job! We have to grow and become bold in spirit! Step out when the Lord calls you to it! Be consumed by His presence so that you can consume others with His love! This beautiful cycle with our Dad begins with surrender, letting go, and building an altar. After that, we move on to waking up every morning, seeing the Road right in front of us, and choosing to walk on it again…and again…and again.

Let's be teachable. Let's be humble. Pride will lead your feet away from the Narrow Road. Jesus does not want to be given a heart that is full of yourself, but a heart that is full of *HIM*self. If all you give Him are actions of worship and prayer on a Sunday morning or Wednesday night, your sight will fade and once again you will lose your way. The beauty of a heart that desires to walk the Narrow Road is a heart that will be rewarded. The greatest reward does not come from your outward decisions that everyone knows about. No! The hardest, sweetest choices you will ever make are hidden within your soul. It is what I like to call "secret place choices". The Father is constantly watching you and me to see how we will respond in the secret places of our hearts when difficulties arise. I am convinced that the decisions that keep us walking steadily are the ones others will never know about.

> *"Your Father who sees what you do in secret will reward you." Matthew 6:4*

We have to choose to walk in His ways. We have to desire to walk on the Road every day. I encourage you, begin your day with surrender. Do not be heavy from the day before if things happened that shouldn't have. Do not be tied to failures. Jesus does not tie you to your past, so why should you do that? You do not have time to regret the things from yesterday.

> *"Stop worrying about tomorrow, because tomorrow will worry about itself. Each day has enough trouble of its own." Matthew 6:34*

So, be here…today! Don't be in yesterday. Don't be in tomorrow. Choose the Road for today! Sometimes women get caught up in the planning and thinking ahead yet somehow still dwell in the past. We are talented creatures! However, we need to become women who dwell in the present in His presence. That is a key to freedom - freedom in Christ! Living in His presence every minute that our lungs take a breath is true freedom! Unfortunately, there have been seasons in my life that I lost sight of this truth. I lost my perspective and did not live in His presence.

In 2012, Ben and I were invited to lead worship for a conference that summer. We felt like the Lord said we should do it, so we obeyed and accepted the invitation. I was very excited because I love to travel! I grew up traveling all around the world! I also love to lead worship with my husband and spend time with my parents, so this made for a perfect trip! But the trip was fourteen days in Kenya! Ben and I had been on trips before, and we were always fine to leave our girls with family or friends if we needed to. We would miss them of course, but I am just making the point that it had never been "difficult" before. I had never left them for two weeks though. So, I began to think and plan and dwell....and what do you know? I am like a bomb ready to explode! I grew so anxious and overwhelmed! Little did I know how much I was going learn on this journey.

At the time, H was three and Ju had just turned one. I was a laid back mom, but Kenya changed all of that. I did not know how fear could literally make someone sick until this season in my life. I was afraid of leaving my daughters. I was afraid of dying. I was afraid of everything. I never understood the word "panic" until those last couple of weeks leading up to the trip. When I would start to think about leaving, my heart would go crazy. It felt like I was about to hyperventilate! I know that sounds dramatic, but it is the truth! I knew I had to start making a change. I knew the Lord was wanting to teach me something, but what was it?!

On Monday morning, before leaving on Saturday, I swung my arms wide open to the Lord and started running after Him. I had to! I would either let fear control me or choose to take control of it...and I was not going to let fear beat me again! So, every night I journaled how I felt that day, and every night I realized the Lord was giving me a key...a key to living. Now, I know what you might be thinking, "Well, I'm not going to Kenya," or "I don't have a problem leaving my kids." Those are just things that brought my

The Narrow Road

issue to the surface. You could be dealing with any number of things, and these keys would apply to you. Just try them. They are to be used to live better, to live free. Since that trip, I try to keep these keys on hand in my spirit. We never come to the end of learning or of needing help along the way. My desire is that you would find hope for your situation and that you would make these keys your own. Let's find things that help us keep our eyes on Him and our feet on the Narrow Road.

The first night that I got into bed and started to journal, I could have thrown up! Fear was crippling me! What if I were going to die on this trip and these were the last days I would spend with my daughters? For the first time that night I also felt like this thought was a gift from the Holy Spirit. What if I knew for sure this was the last week I would have with them? What would I do? What would I say? How would I treat them? How would I parent them differently? What things would I do the same? The list could go on. Too many times we live our lives in "question mode". Honestly, that does not do us any good! In the moment of our emotional collapse, all of our questions seem legitimate. Some might be, but too often we just become controlled by the questions.

Well, here is a question for you! What if we did not live our lives controlled by questions?? No *what if*'s, *but*'s, or *how*'s. If anxiety and fear grip your life, you need to let go of question mode. Living a life bound to all your questions is not living at all. It is not your place to know the mysteries of your life - those are the secrets of your Creator. We are beings designed to trust in a Higher Being. When we fight this and try to plan our lives and figure out all the answers we end up unhappy, unfulfilled, and anxious. You need to slow down just as I needed to slow down.

The first key the Lord showed me was simple…take deep

breaths. I know that phrase may not sound "deep" enough to change your life...but I dare you...I dare you to take control of your mind and emotions when you start to feel like you are spinning out of control. Take deep breaths and let peace settle over you. When everything inside of you wants to have a panic attack because of all the things you are going through...fight back with peace! Breathe in and breathe out for as long as it takes. Don't give up!

What is it in your life that is crippling you? Is it fear? Is it envy? Is it pride? Is it depression? Like I said before, this journey for me was not even about leaving my girls. Leaving them just exposed a place in my heart that had been letting fear grow. Realizing that I did not fully trust the Lord with my life or with my family's life was difficult. No one wants to acknowledge their insecurities. *BUT WE MUST!* The road to freedom starts first with acknowledging what is in your heart. Enough is enough! Don't let the thing that is crippling you thrive in your life. Starve it! Kill it! No matter what it is, it is doing you harm. You first need to take control of your thoughts and breathe.

> *"Whatever is true, whatever is noble, whatever is right, whatever is pure, whatever is lovely, whatever is admirable — if anything is excellent or praiseworthy — think about such things." Philippians 4:8*

It is not about you having enough power on your own to take control. It is about His Spirit in you being lifted higher than any fear or circumstance. You need to keep your thoughts on things

The Narrow Road

that are good and pure, not on fear. When you start having a panic attack because things are just too difficult, or you feel like you will never overcome…just breathe. Breakthrough is coming!

The second day of this journey was terrible!!! Every mistake, every unkind word, every hurtful tone stared at me in the face. Every time I was not the kind of mother I wanted to be, I felt unworthy to be called mom…unworthy of having two amazing daughters…unworthy of the Father's love for me. And if you think that was the worst part of my day, you're wrong! Feeling all of those things was bad enough, but then the Lord decided to use my 3-year-old to teach me my lesson for the day. Sometimes it is difficult to humble ourselves and learn from those we don't see as a "teacher". But the Lord uses whoever, whenever, however He chooses to, and that day He used my daughter.

Every time I treated my daughter wrongly she never lost her peace with me, and I began to be humbled. It felt devastating. I mean, come on! If I am going to blow up, you have to blow up with me, right? During one of my horrible moments she even said, "I forgive you. You being rude." It literally took my breath away. I tried over and over to make a better choice the next time. If I knew this was my last week with her, I would want every minute to count. I would want every situation to be a teaching moment for my daughters and me. I would want to respond in peace and in love. I would want to be a mother and a wife who eats of the fruit of the Spirit and who feeds her children the same.

It was hard to not feel depressed or discouraged, unworthy or condemned. At least I softened enough to take this lesson to heart. I had to be willing to look my mistakes in the face. I want to be a mom, wife, daughter, sister, friend who asks for forgiveness before those around me offer it. Hannah-Brooke offered forgiveness to me, but I still went back to her and asked for it myself. Asking for forgiveness changes something on the inside. If you feel like there needs to be a shift in your life, forgiveness is a great first step. Forgive yourself, forgive others, and also ask to be forgiven. Do not be so proud that you cannot learn a lesson from a small, precious child. The Father loves to use His little ones to teach big things to hearts that will receive.

What things in your life do you need to acknowledge and get rid of? What mistakes do you need to let go of? Who do you need to ask to forgive you? What do you need to forgive yourself from? Too often, we take our mistakes and hide them in a corner only for the purpose of replaying our regrets. By our own choice, we let guilt and shame come in.

The most important thing I did on this day was receive the love and forgiveness from my daughter each time she gave it to me. When our hearts are hard and hurting, sometimes we build walls around us to shut people out. We believe that because of our mistakes we are unlovable. How could anyone love us through our mess? If you haven't heard the good news, I am about to tell you! Jesus not only loved us when we were a mess, but He died for us! His act of love gives us the option to choose love and to have His Spirit dwell within us. He wants to clean up our mess! There is no greater love than His, and He is offering it to you today! Fresh. Pure.

The second key is…receive love. Humble yourself. Let yourself receive somebody's love for you. Let yourself receive *HIS* love for you. Again, that may sound easy, but if your heart is in an unhealthy place, receiving love can be the hardest, best thing for you. We think we are undeserving, but He says differently! We have never gone so far that we are out of the radius of His love. A lot of times, He will love on us through other people. So, humble yourself and receive. Beloved means "you are greatly loved; dear to the heart…a person who is greatly loved." You are His beloved!

"I am my beloved's and my beloved is mine."
Song of Solomon 6:3

By Wednesday, I headed to bed thankful for my day. I was thankful for all that the Lord was teaching me. Earlier that day, I had received several comments from people like "have a great trip", "I'm so excited for you", and "don't worry about things here." All I could think to myself was, "Seriously?" I still could not connect with the excitement of going, and I definitely could not let go of the worry! I put on that fake smile and graciously said thank you to people while on the inside I was sick to the core.

I wanted Wednesday to be my "transition" day. I wanted to feel like I had made a big step emotionally and that I could start getting excited about the trip. I wanted to let go of all the worry, anxiety, and fear that had grown inside of me. I gave myself until mid-week to deal with what I needed to, and then I needed to move on. By the way my day was going I was sure I would not come around before bedtime, but the Father never ceases to amaze me. I honestly went to bed peaceful and even started to anticipate leaving on Saturday.

The third key is…surround yourself with worship. Music is a powerful thing! It goes straight to the heart and touches a deep place. I literally had music playing all day, and it began to shift my perspective. It started to change something in my spirit. Now, don't get me wrong! I enjoy a good country song, but I don't think a song about a broken heart or losing everything was what I needed to fill my spirit up with during that season! It would have been counter-productive and would have only stirred up more fear.

When you are going through challenges, I encourage you to pay attention to what you are listening to. Have worship music playing in your house and in your car. Do not let yourself get away from it! Let it fill you. Music has a way of shifting something from the inside out. It changes the atmosphere around you. Nine times out of ten, my daughters have a better day when I keep worship music playing in the house. They are more peaceful and joyful, and they don't even realize why! It is because I am changing the atmosphere in my home by what I let "fill" it. Fill up your home! Fill up yourself with songs that declare who He is in your life! Soak in songs that cause you to pour out your love on Him and songs that encourage you in His unfailing mercies. Do not get discouraged! Lift up your eyes and see where your help comes from! As you let worship touch your heart, you will find that your heart will touch His.

"I lift up my eyes to the mountains — where does my help come from? My help comes from the Lord!" Psalm 12:1-2

When do you put on that fake smile with people? What is going on in your heart when you feel the need to put on your mask? Decide that a transition needs to be made, and then make choices that help you accomplish it. This worship key can help you on the journey. You have got to start on the inside, and music touches a deep place. Let worship work a shift in your perspective.

The following day seemed to be a much better day. I did not feel quite as overwhelmed with leaving, and I did not let myself indulge in thoughts of fear. Fear is so unpleasant! So, why do so many of us continue to let fear take root in our minds, and grow thoughts that only bring anxiety and unrest?? Fear feeds on a mind and heart that is exhausted, unsure, and unprotected. That is why we are encouraged to

> *"Set your minds on things above, not on earthly things."*
> *Colossians 3:25*

You fuel your fear by believing what it tells you. When you give weight to worry you will find yourself quickly becoming consumed by a fire - a fire that is very real. Fear is real! That is exactly why you have to deal with it quickly. Do not let yourself be tormented! Do not let yourself indulge in those thoughts! At some point, enough is enough!! Think on things *ABOVE*! I dealt with fear for many, many years, so I understand what I am asking you to do…but I am asking anyway…Just. Let. Go. Sometimes we even get so attached to our fear we believe that is just who we are and how we think. But I am here to tell you, "*THERE IS FREEDOM*!"

On this particular day, as I forced myself to control my thoughts, I found my mind wondering about how wonderful it would be to go on this trip with my husband and parents. I wondered about all the things I would see, the people I would meet, and the ways that God might use us. I continued to use the worship key from the day before, and as I would pray I found myself carrying a big heart for the people we were going to meet. I began to feel connected to the heart of why we were going to Kenya in the first place. The key for this day was….think of others. I did not realize it at first but as I would think and pray for the friends we were going meet, I found rest. I realized, *AGAIN*, that I had been putting too much weight on my feelings and was making myself the most important person. I had only been thinking of me, me, me, all week! I made all of my fears and problems more important than other people, and it was time to move on! The moment we take our focus off of ourselves good things always follow.

Take a moment and think about your last few days. Be honest with yourself. Who have you thought about? Could the situation you are in be changed in any way if you would start thinking about others? Don't put the "crown" on your head today. Get out from in front of the mirror and pray for someone else. Is it a friend? Maybe it is an enemy? I must say, this is not the easiest key of the bunch, but it is powerful. So, don't indulge today. Let go. Think of others and see how it changes your life.

Well, one day left. I was still not sure if I was ready. I kept hoping that I would be strong emotionally and not cry very much or at all when I left. I remember heading to bed very nervous about kissing my daughters goodbye. In that moment of leaving I wanted to remember everything that the Lord had taught me through the week. I needed His strength. "My children are not mine," kept running through my head. They are truly His! Any time worry started to creep in I tried to think of how the Heavenly Father would always be with them. I had to ask myself, "Do I really trust the Lord with my daughters? Do I really trust Him with my life?" I wanted to say yes, but the past week had been a challenge to feel that trust.

The key for the last day was…think on scripture. I found great peace in His Word. Just like I did with worship, I surrounded myself with scripture. Write it on your mirror, put it on your fridge, put sticky notes in your car, read it…soak it up all day! There is something about the Word! It is alive! Let it work in your heart. Maybe it is one particular scripture you need to have all over your house or maybe it is a lot of different ones. The Word strengthens our hearts to endure difficult times and thrive through change. The Word comforts us through sorrow and guides us through uncertainty. The Word can be trusted. His Word is faithful. His Word is a bridge built from His heart to ours.

Be open to the scriptures He would give you. Have a soft heart, and be willing to listen. Do not make it difficult. Just open your Bible, and I bet you there will be a scripture just for you on that "random" page. Be faithful to read your scripture all day. Believe what it says to you!

I hope you take hold of these special, simple keys. I hope you journey, the way I did, with a willing heart, letting the Lord work through you! It is not about five steps, twelve steps, or more to freedom! I do not believe there is any magic in these keys the Lord showed me. I do believe they are lessons from the Spirit. They are lessons to be learned and relearned until they become habit. You may have gone in depth with all of the keys, or you may have a particular one that stood out to you. I encourage you to journal your process. It is important to write things down. It will encourage you now and even later down the road. My prayer is that each day you feel encouraged and challenged to press on through your situation. In Him, there is hope and life and freedom!

To recap, the five keys are… #1 - breathe #2 - receive love #3 - surround yourself with worship #4 - think of others #5 - think on scripture. These keys are priceless. Think about your life. What if you used these keys every day?! I mean, *REALLY* used them! What if, when stressful situations came up, you kept your peace because you have learned to breathe? What if, when your heart gets hard, and you want to build walls up to shut people out, that you do the opposite and receive love? What if, because you have filled yourself up with worship, no matter what presses against you, your heart pours out worship? What if, every day you live your life making other people more important than yourself? What if, His

Word meant so much to you that you actually believed what it said and let it work in your life?

These are great *what if*'s but do not let them stay questions. Take a minute, and really think about the situations that you deal with every day. How would your day look differently if you started responding with these keys? It would be life changing! Too many times we blow up at our children, make ourselves the most important, isolate ourselves from others, and mistrust the Lord. It is time to fight against our nature! We fight back not with anger and rage, but with peace and dependency on the Lord.

Use these keys! They are simple and manageable. They are tools! Do not be overwhelmed by them all at once. Do what I did. Focus on one key for one day. Do not rush through it, but linger for a day, process with the Lord, and learn something. Go through the five days as many times as you need. Maybe decide that every six months you are going to do a self-check and evaluate where you are. You might be doing great, or you might see that stress has crept in again. Perhaps fear has started to smother you? If issues have surfaced again, just go through the keys once more. Use them as tools every day.

These keys are like layers. Every time you go through them you will go deeper and see new things. The Lord is always moving and working in more profound ways if you will let Him. He will shine His light in your life if you give Him the chance. Do not be afraid of what is in the dark. You might have a corner with some things you need to acknowledge and get rid of. Be obedient and do so. I know there is also some hidden treasure in the dark! You will find yourself more fulfilled with the light on, exposing both sin and treasure, than you would be by staying in the dark to protect your regrets. He has special gifts for you if you will let Him show you where they are in the room of your heart. He will give you unconditional love, hope, joy, strength, provision, vision, direction, peace, and so much more. He will give you everything! He will be your everything! Go there. Turn the light on. Use the keys. Live your life to the fullest. Live your life in freedom!

Walking closely with the Lord and letting Him strip us of our mask keeps us close to His heart. It keeps us walking the Road. I thought my Kenya lesson was about MacKenzie Myers as a "mom". I was wrong. It was not about learning to leave my girls; it was not about parenting better…it was about MacKenzie Myers as a "daughter of the King". The lesson was in my identity. We have got to learn that if we simply allow the Holy Spirit to work on us as a son or daughter, all other areas will follow along. We do not need something to "fix" us as a mom or wife; we only need to know who we are in Him. We do not need other people to tell us who we are. We need the Word of God and His Spirit living inside of us! If we let our Heavenly Father work on us as His son or daughter first, who we are as a business owner, employee, wife, husband, mother, father, or friend will be in a healthy place too. We just need to know who we are! If we truly know who we are in Him as an individual, we will…

> *"Put on compassion, kindness, humility, gentleness, and patience." Colossians 3:12*

I believe if I had had this revelation before, I would have responded differently about leaving for Kenya. Instead, I put on fear, anxiety, and self-centeredness.

"There is a path that seems straight to someone, but in the end it is a path to death." Proverbs 14:12

We need the Lord to bring revelation. We need to understand that the road that seems straight to us is crook in reality. And that is not a path worthy for our feet to walk on. We must deal with the deepest things in our hearts so we can recognize the difference between the path that leads to death and the Road that leads to life.

CHAPTER 9: PETALS

What a beautiful, beautiful thing it is to journey through every season of our lives with Jesus. My, how I love that name! There is no sweeter name than the name of Jesus. I love how knowing Him changes everything! He changes our identity, our desires, and our destiny. When we were sinners, we walked on a broad road where many others traveled. We would stop on the corner to see what the local merchant had to sell. If we liked it, we would give our treasure for mere items. We would give and give until there was nothing left in our pockets.

The challenge is to see that our treasure is not just our money. Our treasure is also our affection and our time. When we run out of coins, we turn to paying for the worthless with that which holds the greatest worth…our hearts. We start with little pieces of our hearts and think that it will not change us that much. Before we know it, little pieces turn to big, and we find that the Lord does not hold our hearts any longer.

"No one can serve two masters." Matthew 6:24

Our hearts cannot be sold out to the world and sold out for Jesus. If you are sold out to one, you will not have enough to spend on the other. If your life added up to a certain amount of money, I would dare you to be honest and answer these questions. Where are you spending your life? What is important to you?

"Where your treasure is, there your heart will be also."
Matthew 6:21

As Jesus is seeking us out, where will He find us? Will He find us on the corner paying who knows how much for something of no value? Will He find us beautifully poor because we have spent everything on Him? Will He find us walking the Narrow Road? I hope in everything we do, we can make choices that keep our feet steady on the Road.

Challenges come in all shapes and sizes, and some seem more difficult than others. They all have a purpose though. I believe every challenge that comes our way causes us to grow and strengthens our walk. Every challenge has a corresponding revelation. They are just lessons. Look back on trials in your life, and see if you can pinpoint what the Lord was dealing with in your heart. Journal about it if you have not. Writing things down can, many times, bring a greater perspective to the situation.

The Narrow Road

A few weeks before Christmas I had an amazing revelation that came to me! It was not the first time I had this revelation, but in many ways it absolutely felt like it was the first time. I had gotten sick a couple of weeks before Christmas Sunday. At the end of the first week, I started feeling better. I was thankful for that because Ben and I were supposed to sing a special for Christmas. Also, I had just assumed that I would get placed on the worship team that Sunday because I had been off for several weeks.

Monday morning I wake up to find my sinuses freaking out again, and my throat was burning. Tuesday I started coughing. Wednesday, and Thursday I could not speak because I was so hoarse. On Wednesday, I started doing my heart check. How would I feel if I could not sing on Sunday? Did it matter to me? What if Ben decided to do the song with a different vocalist? The questions went on and on. Honestly, it took me by surprise because I had not dealt with anything like this in a long time. Serving on the worship team was just that…serving. It was not about being on the stage or getting the solo for me. I am simply a lover of Jesus and a passionate worshiper. It does not matter to me if I worship from the stage or in the congregation.

So, here I am having these thoughts and a little bit worried about my response. I knew Jesus could do anything so if He wanted me to sing He would heal me. I started breaking down my questions to try to figure out if it did matter to me, why? I was driving to the studio one day processing all this again, and it hit me. Finally, I could pinpoint what that little lie was trying to work in my heart. If Jesus could heal me but chose not to, then it must be true — Jesus does not need me. Before I could even let the thought take root, I heard the smallest voice in the back of my head say, "But that is not my worth to Him." I heard it over and over. The louder it got, the more I cried with joy. It was as if that phrase was put in my heart by His Spirit for me to fight back with. I just kept saying, "That is not my worth to Him. That is not my worth to Him."

As I said, it is not like I had not had this revelation before. I knew I could not earn my entrance into Heaven. It is not about works because it is about His grace. What Jesus did on the cross for me is a gift if I choose to receive it. I know it is not about what I can do for the Lord. But, over the last couple of months, the Lord has been taking me deeper into that revelation. Revelation brings maturity. I think as we grow, our stories change, and our revelations deepen. This situation was a fresh revelation that brought a greater maturity to my soul.

The first freeing thought was the honesty with myself that Jesus did not "need" me. He is God and Ruler of all, and I am not so mighty in His eyes that He cannot get something done without me. However, I am loved in His eyes, and many times He does ask me to do things. In those moments, I am simply a daughter ministering alongside her Heavenly Dad. It is not because of anything I have accomplished. A Dad just likes to use His kids. We need to let go of the extra weight that we put on ourselves.

"For His yoke is easy and His burden is light."

Matthew 11:30

Whatever He has called us to should not cause unrest. I always remember something that my Mom told me when I was a little girl. I was struggling with a decision, and she said, "If you don't feel like you have a direct word from the Lord, let Peace guide you. He is the Prince of Peace." Let Him be your peace. If you are walking in an identity that puts the weight of the world on

The Narrow Road

you, maybe something needs to be adjusted.

I believe we walk a fine line when trying to understand the fear of the Lord. Knowing that He can literally do whatever He wants, whenever He wants and does not need us can be overwhelming. At the same time that we are not anything to Him, we are everything to Him. That is the fine line. If we are not careful, we can get in a bad place of feeling like our purpose on earth is not valid. We start to believe we are not truly loved or wanted by the Being who created us. It is not about feeling unwanted. It is about Him revealing His overwhelming love for us! Though He does not need us, He wants us! We are His joy! For us, He came to earth and lived and died. His desire is to have a relationship with us. How precious is that?!

We were created in His image and we are so loved! I knew in this fresh revelation that my Father loved me, for me. Just me. He does not love me because I sing. He does not love me because I own a business. He does not love me because I dance. He does not love me because I mother and keep my house clean. He does not love me because I teach. He does not love me because I act. It does not matter to Him if I worship from the stage or my row. I worship the same no matter where I am standing, and He knows my heart. My worship is not any more valuable to Him if it is given from the stage, and it is not any less valuable if given from my chair. I am of great value to Him!

That Sunday was one of the most freeing Sundays I had felt in a long time. I was not better. I did not sing. I was peaceful and satisfied being His Princess. Vanity and fame were knocking, but buying what they offered cost too much. Insecurities cost my identity. I stood that Sunday with my feet steady on the Narrow Road. I knew who I was, and I was content. I did not want to make an exchange with the world. The only one I want to exchange with is Jesus. I want to continually exchange my current revelation for a greater revelation. I want to exchange my plans for His plans.

"'For I know the plans I have for you,'
declares the Lord." Jeremiah 29:11

And they are far better than anything we could ever plan for ourselves. I know this is a hard question, but what are the things that you hold too closely? What things do you do that make you feel valued to the Lord? Is it how you run your home or business? Is it how you can perform? Is it in your looks? Remember when the Lord asked me to change the way I forgive? I think He wants us to change the way we hear Him say, "I love you." I think too many times we convince ourselves that He says, "I love you BECAUSE…" We start to believe that He has to have a reason to love us. That is a lie! His love is pure and perfect. He offers it willingly! He simply says, "I love you." There is no "because". There is nothing for us to live up to. There is not a to-do list that we have to accomplish ever day. He just loves us.

Imagine yourself sitting outside with a perfect blue sky above and soft, green grass at your feet. There are countless flowers all around you. Suddenly you hear, "Pick one." You pick one, and He says, "Pull the petals." You know as you pull the petals that you are supposed to say the little phrases that go along with it. Your heart is unsettled because if He asked you to do that then He knows there is a chance you will end on the petal of "not". How could He do that to you? How could He toss you aside?

With tears beginning to burn in your eyes, you pick the first petal. "He loves me." The next, "He loves me not." You toss another. "He loves me. Shew, I made it to love again," goes through

The Narrow Road

your thoughts. You move on to the next petal and the next. Petals are tossed all around as well as your emotions. You are getting to the end and with the final petal tossed to the ground, your heart stops. "He loves me no…" But, before you could finish your word, you feel Him wrap His hands around yours.

His hands were so big that you could not even see your hand that held the remaining, naked stem. His hands were also rough because He was the gardener of the field where you sat. He constantly worked to pull the weeds that sought to grow and destroy what He had made. He searched for sticks and rocks to rid the field of them. He would feed the soil and water the seeds. He was constantly at work. He never slept. He was steady and faithful in all His ways.

So, how could He leave you unloved? There you sat with feelings of brokenness creeping in. His beautiful eyes pierced yours, and you hear His soft voice, "Beloved, what are you doing?" He opens His hands, and where you held just a stem, there was once again a flower. "Let's start over," He says. You could not bear going through this again, but even with uncertainty in your heart there was hope that just maybe your last petal would uncover a different answer.

To your surprise, the Gardner reaches for the first petal Himself and tosses it to the ground. "I love you." Your chest feels heavy, and you cannot breathe. Saying the next phrase, "He loves me not," is hard enough to do yourself, but now to hear Him say it out loud was just going to be unbearable. And how many times would you have to hear it before getting to the last petal? You prayed for grace. He reaches for the second petal. With a smile on His face, His lips spoke, "I love you more." You are in shock. He tosses the third pedal. "Here comes the 'not.' That was just a trick," you say to yourself, but still the same answer came. The fourth pedal hits the ground. "I love you more." The fifth is tugged from the stem. "I love you more." The sixth. "I love you more!" The moment was overwhelming, and your face is washed with endless tears. He pulls the seventh petal and shouts, "I love you more!" You are sitting, disillusioned with what is happening. The Gardener pulls the eighth and final petal and with even more excitement declares, "I love you more!"

There you are, just as you suspected. Broken. But not because of hurt or disappointment. You had never known the brokenness of love before, but there you wept, broken, soft because of His overwhelming love. With every "I love you more" layers of hurt and insecurities, lies about who you are were being broken off of you. His strong arms gently lifted you from the ground so you could see the vast field. It had no end. "With every flower you will know more and more of my love for you. You will never get to the end!" He laughs with joy, "An endless field where countless flowers bloom, yes, this is my love for you!"

The eyes of your heart began to open. Warmth floods your soul and joy comes over you like you have never known. "Come back as often as you want. Pick as many flowers as you want. You will never run out! Let the petals be a testimony to remind you of who you are and how I love you. Don't be trapped by other lovers in this world. What they offer has limits, but My love knows no bounds. I am the Lover of your soul, the Gardener of your heart." Leaving a kiss on your mouth He tenderly smiles and walks away.

Peace settles upon you, and before you realize it you are running through the field breathing in every beautiful fragrance. Diving to the ground, you realize you are doing something you haven't done in a while…you're laughing. With a beautiful smile now on your face, you look around at the countless flowers. Picking one near you, you toss the first petal. "He loves me." The Gardener watches from a distance with great delight and love in His heart. The reach for the second petal took trust, and more than anything you wanted to believe. It was time to change the way you thought about His love for you. It was time to trust! You looked all around and saw endless beauty and life, and for the first time you began to understand. The Love that first had to break you, now made you whole. With His perfect blue sky above, and knees knelt in the soft, green grass, your words began to flow through the air… "He loves me more."

How I pray that we could grasp the endless love He has for us.

"I love you with an everlasting love. So I will continue to show you my kindness." Jeremiah 31:3

His love goes on and on and on! His kindness breaks our walls down. His kindness softens us to repentance. His kindness shows us how to live every day in His amazing love. He is constantly at work in our hearts.

"Indeed, He who watches over Israel will neither slumber nor sleep." Psalms 121:4

His desire for us is to experience the power of the cross and to live in the victory He won over the grave! We are no longer unloved and unknown!

> *"My Beloved has gone down to His garden...to browse in the garden. I am my Beloved's and my Beloved is mind."*
>
> Song of Solomon 6:2-3

He walks the garden of our hearts every day longing for us to know the depth of His love. We are not only known by Him, but we are also loved! We build walls in our hearts that keep us from living in the fullness of His love. I pray that we would let Love soften us and tear down those walls. I pray that we would let Him work the soil of our hearts. I pray that we would be able to trust, and with every petal know that He loves us more. Walking in the revelation of His love teaches our hearts to be content. It is living life in the contentment of who we are in Him that keeps us journeying on the Narrow Road.

CHAPTER 10: BONES TO BREATH

I pray that every day you would see the beautiful Narrow Road before you. I pray that you would see where your feet are stepping with every decision you choose, every thought you think, and every action you make. Draw near to Him, and He will give you strength.

"The Lord is my strength and my shield. My heart trusts Him...The Lord is His people's strength..."

Psalm 28:7 & 8

We are faced with so much every day. I cannot help but see the Road in front of me with every thought I think and in everything I do. This is absolutely real for me. This is the way I live my life. For example, I finished my work week at the studio last Thursday, and on Friday I got crazy sick. I had the flu and had to stay home all week. A few days later, I also came down with strep and that kept me home for another week. Two full weeks stuck at home! Not fun. My hope was that I would be functioning again by our company rehearsals at the studio this week, but I did not succeed.

I saw the Road when I realized that I was not going to make rehearsals. My choice appeared quickly before me as I thought about all the things I would miss out on. Anxiety likes to sneak into my life really quickly. I saw the Road when I also realized I would be missing my pointé class! What if they started the recital piece? What if I do not get a great part because I am not there? I saw the Road again when I accepted the fact that I would not be going to dance at the Smoky Mountain Opry that week either.

The Opry is a beautiful theater located about an hour away from where I live. Zion Dance Company had the privilege of learning some of their choreography when they came to the studio. Two weeks later we were supposed to work that choreography on their stage for them. It was going to be a great experience, as well as a whole lot of fun! In the sixty seconds that we decided I was still too sick to dance, all kinds of scenarios stared at me in the face. Deep down, I knew I could not dance. My body was still extremely weak, and my heart was very disappointed. What was I going to do with that disappointment?

I am just being real honest with you. If I were the same person I was a year ago, I would have had a pity party. Woe is me! How come I am the one that got sick? What is going to happen at all the rehearsals and dance classes without me? People are going to start thinking I am not needed. If I do not get to dance at the Opry, people might think all the other dancers are better than me. Shew, just writing that out makes me sick to my stomach! Anyone

The Narrow Road

who thinks like that produces a heavy and depressed heart. However, I am resting here on my couch, blessed with His peace. I got sick because sometimes that just happens. If I do not get a great part in the recital piece, I bless the dancer who does. If people say that I am not needed or that I am the worst dancer, that is ok. I know who I am in Christ, and my worth to Him does not change. That is how I walk the Narrow Road. I made those Narrow Road decision about an hour ago. I am not anxious. I am not struggling. I am at rest.

I am a new creation. I do not live the same way, and I definitely do not think the same way I did even from several months ago. I have been on this amazing journey of pursuing Christ in a whole new way. As I have been asking for revelation of what it means to walk the Narrow Road, sometimes my Heavenly Dad puts these little tests out in front of me. They are little heart checks for me to see where I am walking.

Today, I made the choice to care for my body the way I needed to. I did not let insecurities control me. As I have walked this Road today, I do not just feel my Father with me now…I *KNOW* that He is here with me. I know the Road I chose today led me closer to the Father. I did not choose a road that led me to my own selfish desires or indulged in my insecurities.

This whole process is bigger than me! It affects me as well as those around me. The Narrow Road looked like me choosing to honor my fellow company members and being secure in who I am in Christ. It looked like me choosing to bless and not to curse. I am certain that if I did not have His Word hidden in my heart, today would have been more difficult. This passage encouraged me to see things as Jesus does and to walk better.

"Give us the bread that we need for today." Matthew 6:11

That verse is all I needed today to keep my heart in a pure place before the Lord. My Father was faithful to give me the bread that I needed for *THIS* day. He satisfied my soul with His food, and I did not need to go searching for anything else. I did not need anyone to pity me. I did not need them to reschedule the Smoky Mountain Opry date. I did not need any of that because my appetite was full on Jesus.

Of course, I am sad. I do not think Jesus expects us to go through things and not feel disappointment or sadness. He just wants us to be careful what we do with those emotions. Do you ever have days like I have had? My body is exhausted from being sick, and my spirit could have grown exhausted too if I had chosen differently. Are you weary and discouraged because of something going on in your life? Does it feel like, on top of exhaustion, the Lord just doesn't give you a break? Situation after situation you are faced again with choosing Him or choosing yourself. It is a constant process, and He is there with you! In your weakness, He can be your strength.

"My grace is all you need. My power works best in weakness." 2 Corinthians 12:9

His power works best when we are weak. I do not know about you, but I want to see His power working in my life. What I could accomplish on my own is nothing compared to what Jesus' power could accomplish in me.

It is when we are weak and dry, and honestly just plain dead, that Jesus comes in and does a beautiful work in our lives. The story from Ezekiel 37 has become one that is constantly changing how I think about life and how I live it. The vision starts off with the prophet saying,

"The Lord set me down in the middle of a certain valley."
Ezekiel 37:1

I started asking this question to myself. What certain valley has the Lord set me down in? Where has He set you? When we look out, what things in our lives look dead to us? What places in our lives and hearts seem to be dried up? When we look at circumstances in our lives, do we trust God fully? Or do we think we know what the best plan is for our lives? Do we think we can revive ourselves from being dried up bones? The Lord asked Ezekiel, "Human one, can these bones live again?" Jesus is asking us this same question. I hope we have soft hearts and enough fear of the Lord in our souls to respond the way Ezekiel did,

"Lord God, only You know." Ezekiel 37:3

If our lives are not a mystery to us, maybe we have not fully surrendered them to Christ.

"He said to me, 'Prophesy over these bones and say to them..." Ezekiel 37:4

When Jesus is working in our hearts, He will often use us in the process of completing that work. He is like a parent who is trying to teach a lesson to His child. Let's say that I am trying to teach my daughters how to stretch and work out so they can become strong dancers. If I am the only one who puts forth the effort and all they ever do is watch me, their muscles will never become strong. Their bodies will never become flexible. I have to draw them in and encourage them to participate. This is the same lesson our Heavenly Dad is trying to teach us. We have to participate with the Holy Spirit so our bodies can become strong, and we can reap the rewards of what we have worked hard for.

My daughters cannot be strong because I am strong. I can be their strength when they are weak, and I would always desire to help them along the way. However, it is crucial that they build their own strength. They cannot be called a Christian just because I am a Christian. That is why even now I pull them close to me and encourage them to participate with me in prayer, worship, and reading His Word. I want them to start building their spiritual muscles so that, one day, they will choose to follow Jesus because that is what they want to do. I want to help them see the different paths. I want to live a life that shows them the fruit of walking the Road more narrow.

I would ask you two questions. How can you build strength in your own spirit? How can you "work out" your spiritual muscles? If you ever want to help anybody on their journey, you must first know how to strengthen yourself. You have to learn how it feels to live a life of conviction. Ask the Lord for creative ways to strengthen who you are on the inside. Lean on Him and His wisdom.

> *"Trust in the Lord with all your heart; do not depend on your own understanding." Proverbs 3:5*

Trust what He says to you! Obey what He speaks to you. The actions that will strengthen your spirit are actions of foolishness in the world's eye. Do not let that stop you! The world is not your standard!

Another question I would ask is this. How can you build strength in others? Think about your week. Where did you go? Who did you see? How could you strengthen those people? If we say others are more important than ourselves how are we showing that? There could be many opportunities for us to strengthen someone if we would be brave enough to look for those moments. Take the chance. Be brave.

Ezekiel was brave. The Lord said for him to prophesy over an entire valley of bones. That seems like a pretty hopeless situation to be prophesying over. But, he trusted in the Lord more than himself, and he obeyed. Part of what the Lord had Ezekiel prophesy was this,

> *"When I put breath in you, and you come to life, you will know that I am the Lord." Ezekiel 37:6*

I began to ponder and ask the Lord to reveal something to me in this specific verse. What I found to be true, for myself anyway, is once our bones are "put back together" we become complacent. We think that is enough. Or maybe we think it is when we have flesh on our bones again that we have reached some success, and we are done. It says,

"Bones came together, bone by bone. When I looked, suddenly there were sinews on them. The flesh appeared, and then they were covered over with skin. But there was still no breath in them." Ezekiel 37:7-8

Where have we become satisfied with just our bones coming together? Have we become content in our flesh that we do not even yearn for His breath? We have to ask ourselves, "Am I settling for bones and skin? Is that all I need? Is that good enough for me?" Bones and flesh are not bad! They are good and much needed. Too often, we overstep their significance and see them as the reward when really that is only the beginning of what God has promised! Even things that are "good" are not always God's best for us. His best is for us to be filled with His breath and have life - abundant life! When He takes us from bones to breath is when we know that He alone is Lord. He is the Lord and all life comes from Him!

"The Lord, created the Heavens and stretched them out.

The Narrow Road

He created the earth and everything in it. He gives breath to everyone, life to everyone who walks the earth."

Isaiah 42:5

Jesus is the breath in our lungs; He is the life in our bodies. For me, it is not enough anymore to be bones or flesh that appear to be living. Having the appearance of "living" and actually walking with His breath inside our bodies are very different things. I think that is the battle in so many of our lives. We have these dead places inside that we have masked with flesh, and we call it living. How I pray that we would let the Lord come in and stir us to prophesy! At this point in the passage of scripture all the bones were together, sinews had appeared, and flesh covered the skeletons…but they were all still laying there. It was because,

"There was still no breath in them." Ezekiel 37:8

It makes my heart grieve when I think that God would look down on us and say, "There is still no breath in them." I want to be asking the Lord to breathe in me every morning that His faithfulness lets me open my eyes! I want my passion for Him to be stirred up every day by His breath flowing through my spirit! If I am crazy, then I am crazy! But I am never going back to my former life and the old way of thinking! I am *FULLY* convinced that Jesus lives in me and I in Him!

> *"Yes, I am the vine; you are the branches. Those who remain in Me, and I in them, will produce much fruit."*
> *John 15:5*

I believe that verse with all my heart! This is what John 15:5 sounds like to me, "Yes! Jesus is in me, and I am in Him! If I will stay with Him on the Narrow Road then He will do good through my life!" I can be the one that He uses to show Himself to people if I stay in Him - *IF* I will walk this Narrow Road. I am convinced that He wants to use me and allows me to succeed because of His kingdom!

> *"He was fully convinced that God is able to do whatever He promises."*
> *Romans 4:21*

Let that be said of us! When we still see only lifeless flesh laying on the ground, let it be said that we were fully convinced that the Lord would fulfill His promises. Life with Jesus is walked out by faith. There is no other way. Faith is what pleases the heart of God.

> *"It is IMPOSSIBLE to please God without faith."*
> *Hebrews 11:6*

Even if there are promises unfulfilled in your life, have faith! It may be a process, but when God speaks, have faith and courage to trust Him. Obey and speak out what He has said to you. Prophesy in the process. Sometimes Jesus will ask us to be persistent and pray something over and over. That does not mean our first prayer was not heard or that it was not effective. I sometimes think the Father is simply looking for His children not to give up. The Father wants His children to be consistent and come to Him with their requests. Are you not a daughter? Ask Him! He loves to hear your voice. He asked Ezekiel to prophesy a second time,

"Say to the breath, the Lord God proclaims: Come from the four winds, breath! Breathe into those dead bodies and let them live." Ezekiel 37: 9

Man! I wish I could put exclamation points in that verse because that just gets me excited beyond words! What a prophetic word! It was time for a promise to be fulfilled. It was time for breath and life to enter those dead bodies! Ezekiel did as the Lord commanded and

"When the breath entered them, they came to life and stood on their feet, an extraordinarily large company."
Ezekiel 37:10

Come on now! We need Jesus to bring His breath from the four winds and breathe into us! We need Him to raise dead parts of our hearts back to life again! And if that was not enough, Jesus looked on the ones who were now living and had compassion on them. Jesus heard them crying out.

"Our bones are dried up, and our hope has perished. We are completely finished." Ezekiel 37:11

If there is one thing I know about Jesus, it is that He does not barely make it to the finish line…He crushes it in record time! Do not lose hope in whatever your circumstances are! Do not become discouraged in your struggles. With everything in you, know that Jesus has your very best in mind. It is another thing I am fully convinced of! Why? Because my Bible tells me so!

"But in all these things we win a sweeping victory through the one who loved us." Romans 8:37

When I think about the Lord looking at His people and having compassion, I picture Him as a runner. He is finishing the final lap and can now see the finish line. He is already in first place, but He does not slow down one bit. He pushes on even harder in order to win a sweeping victory for you! He would never give up or slow down on you. When He sees that finish line, He sees you! He is thinking, "Wow! I cannot wait to show my Beloved what I am about to do for her! I cannot wait to show her My faithfulness! Just you wait, Beloved. Wait and see what I am going to do!"

The bodies are now standing on their feet, and Jesus says to Ezekiel,

"So now, prophesy and say to them, 'The Lord God proclaims: I'm opening your graves! I will raise you up from your graves, My people, and I will bring you to Israel's fertile land. You will know that I am the Lord, when I open your graves and raise you up from your graves, my people. I will put My breath in you, and you will live. I will plant you on your fertile land, and you will know that I am the Lord. I've spoken, and I will do it. This is what the Lord says.'" Ezekiel 37:12-14

WOOHOOOO!!! YAH, GOD! If that does not get your spirit dancing, I do not know what will! What a mighty victory we receive when we accept our adoption from the King! I told you it would be a sweeping victory just like the Word said! The dry bones went from being nothing to having flesh, standing, receiving breath, and being raised up out of the valley! They were raised up out of that grave! They were put on fertile land and made to prosper! Jesus wants to show Himself off for you! That is why we cannot get caught up in thinking that His whole plan was just to bring bones together! He had so much more planned! We cannot settle for less. No, we have to believe and cry out for His breath! I want to desire nothing less than the full plan of receiving breath from the living God!

So, as you have been reading and pondering, what bones do you have in your life? Where do they come from? Do you know? Are you ready to let Christ work through you? Let Him fulfill this Ezekiel passage in your life. Are your bones dead dreams, dead emotions, decayed hope, dried up relationships? Have faith! Let His Spirit come upon you and lead you to that certain valley. Let Him stir in you the gift of prophecy. Look out over those places and know that the Lord stands there with you. Take courage and speak light into the dark. Speak potential into the non-existent. Speak life where there is death, breath where there is emptiness. Have faith that there is a

"God who gives life to the dead and calls things that don't exist into existence." Romans 4:17

Jesus wants to go above and beyond for you if you will trust and walk by faith. Let your faith touch His heart today. The Lord brought bones together, put flesh on them, and breathed into them because He saw His people with compassion. He did not see dry bones. He saw potential. He saw a large company. When He looks at you, He does not see dry bones; He sees potential. He restored His people so they might know that He is Lord. He works His wonders for His own name to be known.

The Narrow Road

"I've spoken and I will do it." Ezekiel 37:14

And He will do it for you!

CHAPTER 11: THE TREASURE OF WAITING

So, we have talked a lot about walking the Narrow Road. I have shared story upon story of how sin presents itself to me. I have also shared how the Narrow Road presents itself with the choice to walk toward the Father or away from Him. In my life, if you have not figured it out, they present themselves — all the time. The choices are always there. It is really precious to me that I get to make those choices every day. I have lived 27 years of my life thinking that I knew Jesus and what it meant to follow Him. I did not have a clue. The story of the dry bones is very dear to my heart. Recently, my Mom asked me what I felt like the Lord had been working on in my life. The best way I could explain it to her was by reading that passage from Ezekiel.

Through my recent journey with the Lord, I could almost feel His promises pulling my bones back together. There were moments in my quiet time that I could sense my flesh being restored, but there was still a season of standing on my feet —

The Narrow Road

breathless. I just waited patiently and prophesied when the Lord stirred it in my heart.

> *"If we look forward to something we don't yet have, we must wait patiently and confidently."* Romans 8:25

So, I waited and remained peaceful and steady. Thankfulness is a good medicine in times of waiting. Too often, when we get stuck in a season of waiting, we decide to take the Writer's pen right out of His hand. I know I have said it in this book before, but I will say it again! Discontentment leads us off the Narrow Road. Discontentment waits at our door, fighting to get in when we are in seasons of waiting. It knows that we will get weary in the waiting. It knows that we will eventually start to open our door hoping to see our promise fulfilled. But opening the door of discontentment is not because of our faith, it is because of our impatience.

We take that pen and start to write our own story. His story for us may not always look like what we want, but I know His story for our lives will be more beautiful and more rewarding than anything we could ever dream. His story for our lives might also be more difficult, but that is just part of it.

In a very long season of my life, when I grew increasingly impatient with the Lord, I learned a valuable lesson. The unexpected pages of my story came one day as I found myself in Psalms 136, the "give thanks" chapter. Up until that day, I could not see His faithfulness. I could not see it in the day before, the week before, the month before, and I was weary. I could not see Him as a good Dad. I could not be thankful. But

"The night is far gone; the day is at hand..." and I, MacKenzie Brooke Myers, *"...will cast off the works of darkness and put on the armor of Light."* Romans 13:12

That day I said to my soul, *"IT IS WELL!"* I looked up to the Heavens and shouted, *"I LOVE YOU!"* I sang a song of thankfulness from my heart! After I had read Psalm 136, it was like everything shifted in my perspective. I was inspired to write my own 136th chapter. So, that day I sat down and did the unexpected. The day before I did not know that the pages of my story were about to change. I had become impatient and ungrateful. I was quite pleased with having the pen of my life in my own hand. On that unexpected day, I did not know what pages would be written about my life, but I was thankful that they did not read the same as the days and weeks before. Thankfulness can bring a twist to your story if you allow it to. In an impatient and self-seeking world, thankfulness is like hidden treasure.

I am encouraging you to write your own 136th chapter. Sit quietly, and let your heart ponder. Let your heart remember all that the Lord has done for you. There are 26 verses in that chapter in Psalms. Start there. Thankfulness changes everything! Just think of what the Lord might do for us, His daughters, if He finds us overflowing with thanksgiving toward Him as our Dad. Let's be vulnerable and real with one another. I am not asking you to do something that I did not do myself. That is why I am willing to show my sincerity and let you read the chapter I wrote. I pulled this from my journal, and nothing was changed. I am being as real with you as I can. I want it to bless you and stir your heart until your own thankfulness bursts forth!

My Own 136

1. Give thanks to the One who brought me and Ben together.
2. Give thanks to the One who gave us two beautiful daughters.
3. Give thanks to the One who has provided for us financially in every time of need.
4. Give thanks to the One who has restored family relationships.
5. Give thanks to the One who has anointed our worship through every good and tough season.
5. Give thanks to the One who provided a job for Ben in April before we got married that August.
6. Give thanks to the One who protects our businesses.
7. Give thanks to the One who provided money for Ben's passport.
8. Give thanks to the One who gives Holy Spirit inspired creativity for choreography.
9. Give thanks to the One who carries my burdens.
10. Give thanks to the One who cared for me through both of my pregnancies.
11. Give thanks to the One who leads me through the desert.
12. Give thanks to the One who loves me through my parents.
13. Give thanks to the One who has birthed songs and dances from my heart.
14. Give thanks to the One who works behind the scenes.
15. Give thanks to the One who has provided for our family a house full of furniture that we did not pay for.
16. Give thanks to the One who has provided for us to drive good vehicles.
17. Give thanks to the One who has given us family all over the world.
18. Give thanks to the One whose presence dwells in my home.
19. Give thanks to the One who watches over my husband and cares for him.

The Treasure of Waiting

20. Give thanks to the One who gives wisdom and strategy and parents with me.
21. Give thanks to the One who has protected us on many flights.
22. Give thanks to the One who came into my heart when I lived in Russia.
23. Give thanks to the One who worked in my heart in South Africa.
24. Give thanks to the One who has given me a gift to write, dance, sing, and manage for His glory.
25. Give thanks to the One who gave us the home we live in.
26. Give thanks to the One who has changed my story.

Even in times of waiting, we should always find our place of thankfulness. We should find our difficult situations to be the perfect time to overflow with a heart of thanksgiving! Take some time with the Lord and think back. Remember when He showed Himself faithful in your life. Do not try to think about all 26 things at once. Just start with number one and let the Holy Spirit bring back each moment to you. You may write down things that surprise you because you never saw them as something to be thankful for or as evidence of His goodness. I know a few things I wrote down surprised me. It delighted my heart to take the time to thank Jesus for what He had done in my life.

Now, this book will always be here, but you do not want to miss what God might be doing in your heart. Drop the book, and go write your own chapter! I guarantee when you come back you will be filled with His joy!

I have a blog called *MacKenzie at Heart* where I share different thoughts, and this revelation of thankfulness is one of the topics I have posted about. Just as I encouraged you, I encouraged all who read my blog to write their own 136th chapter. I started seeing a few people post on Facebook that they had spent some time

139

The Narrow Road

reflecting and writing their thankful chapter. It was moving to see how God was touching lives. Every time I saw #myown136, my heart danced for joy! *My Own 136* can change this world if we will truly live what we believe and never let thankfulness be far from our lips.

Just a week or so after I had this encounter with Jesus about Psalms 136, I was stirred to write another chapter! My second chapter was completely different from the first. It did not have the same feel to it all. The entire chapter focused on people in my life. I was thankful for those around me! The theme and focus of your chapter may change from time to time, and that is wonderful! Thankfulness should never stop! Let's be women and men who overflow with praise for our Father and declare His goodness every where we go! His very Word commands us to

"Be thankful in all circumstances, for this is God's will for you who belong to Christ Jesus." 1 Thessalonians 5:18

If we belong to Christ then we are to imitate Christ. I see the Narrow Road every moment of every day. I am just one person trying to live my life as Jesus wants me to. I wonder in what ways does the Narrow Road present itself to you? You live an entirely different life than I do! We could be complete opposites, but His ways never changes. Thankfully, it does not matter if we have similar lives and characteristics or if we are as different as night and day. Jesus gives us the same tools to help us stay steady on His Road.

When our actions, thoughts, and emotions are about to explode, let's use the guidelines Christ gave us to help us choose the path less traveled. I am not saying we will always make the right decision every time. However, if we will get His Word planted down deep in our hearts, it will begin to take root, and the choosing will become more and more like second nature. Choosing love keeps our feet on the Narrow Road.

"Love is patient, love is kind, it isn't jealous, it doesn't brag, it isn't arrogant, it isn't rude, it doesn't seek its own advantage, it isn't irritable, it doesn't keep a record of complaints, it isn't happy with injustice, but it is happy with the truth." 1 Corinthians 13:4-6

Now, that is a big definition of what love is! That is also why we have to read it every day! We have to saturate ourselves with this verse so that it might start to flow from our lives. Think about the moments in which you want to be impatient. I will just be honest with you, this was a difficult one for me, especially when I am in heavy traffic! But, now I know better, don't I?! If I love the way Jesus taught me, I will not become impatient with the other drivers on the road! If I know that the choice to have patience is the choice that keeps me on the Narrow Road, why would I want to choose differently?

Let's think about the moments in which we think too highly of ourselves. Because of His Word we now know that pride leads to destruction, and humility leads to the Father. So, what do we want to choose?

> *"Conduct yourselves with all humility, gentleness, and patience." Ephesians 4:2*

Another passage that encourages humility along with other traits is this…

> *"Put on compassion, kindness, humility, gentleness, and patience." Colossians 3:12*

Humility is a characteristic of Christ that we are to imitate. Oh, snap! If I were you, I would maybe start to hate me right now. This stuff is hard! Press in and run forward! Let's do this together! Let's find in His Word other traits that might help us make better choices.

> *"But the fruit of the Spirit is love, joy, peace, patience, kindness, goodness, faithfulness, gentleness, and self-control. There is no law against things like this." Galatians 5:22*

We have already learned about some of those, like patience and gentleness. Self-control was a new one. Yikes! I can think of one million and one times that I want to lose my temper with my kids. I see that choice before me and sometimes I have the grace to choose self-control but sometimes I fail. I have felt the reward of choosing self-control, but I still have not figured out how to choose it every time. The thing that always brings me back to the Narrow Road is asking for my daughters' forgiveness. It is that humility thing again. If we will humble ourselves and allow the Lord to help us grow by using our mistakes, then we will find that our feet are firmly back on the right path. Forgiveness is one of the hardest choices I think that presents itself to us. It is not just about forgiving the easy stuff. It is about forgiving when it is difficult and forgiving those that feel like the enemy.

> *"Forgive us our sins, as we forgive those who sin against us." Matthew 6:12*

We are to be walking examples of how Christ has forgiven us. How do we know that forgiving is a "narrow road" quality? Because we have learned it from the Word.

> *"Be kind, compassionate, and forgiving to each other..." Ephesians 4:32*

That is why it is so important to read His Word. We have to devour it and let it change us. It is our road map! Through these scriptures, we have added a few more qualities to our list that help us walk a better way. I like to see things clearly laid out in front of

The Narrow Road

me. So, let's do that together now. These are the qualities that I have taken as treasures.

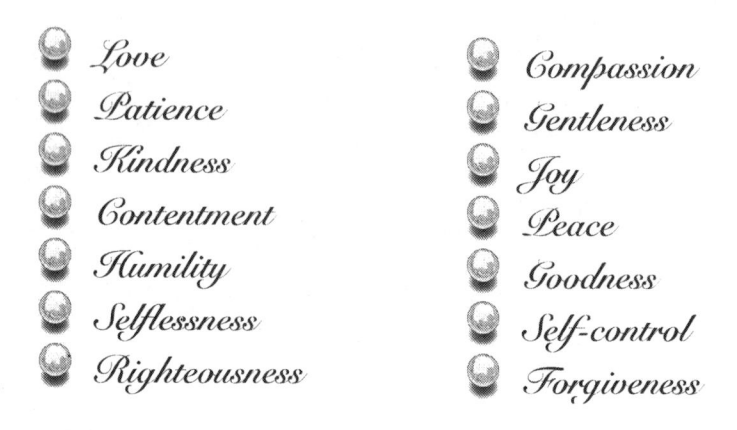

- Love
- Patience
- Kindness
- Contentment
- Humility
- Selflessness
- Righteousness

- Compassion
- Gentleness
- Joy
- Peace
- Goodness
- Self-control
- Forgiveness

All of these things are keys to walking the Narrow Road. We cannot walk there in our own strength. We are imperfect people made perfect in His image. We are called to walk better - we are called to walk like Him! Christ has given us examples of His character. If we can walk through our lives being a reflection of those qualities, then not only will our lives change, but those around us will also change.

I hope you have marked pages in this book or have written down some of the different things that I have shared with you. My heart's prayer is that you have found some tools you can use as you go about your day. Practical tools. I hope you have found useful and creative tools that will strengthen you and encourage you in your walk.

Maybe you are going to write a one year journal for your fiancé or husband. If you do, I bless you on that journey! I pray that God speaks to you and moves in your heart every day as you are faithful to write. Maybe you are in a season of life that the five keys I shared about in chapter eight are becoming helpful tools in your hand. If you are using those keys, I am praying for you on that journey! Perhaps your heart is still back in chapter three, and you are working on the things that you need to let go of. I encourage you, release those things to the Father and build your altar. There is life and reward on the other side of the Gate. I know you can do it!

With Jesus as my best friend, I know I will continue on my journey. Over these past months as His Word has come to life and brought revelation, I feel like I am finally walking around with the lights turned on. Sometimes I do not think we realize we are walking around in the darkness until we have seen a beam of the Light. I know my life will never be the same. Jesus has branded me for Himself, and there is nothing that can compare to His seal of adoption. I want Him to constantly tell me who I am in His eyes and teach me His ways. I also want the same for you!

Living my life knowing who I am in Christ leaves me quite content. I do not need my fears and insecurities. I do not need my walls and hurts. I do not need the distractions and emptiness the world offers. The world is constantly trying to make an exchange with me. The world wants me to buy its goods with my identity as payment. But, I have learned to hold my identity as a priceless gift from my Father. I only want what He offers me. I just need Him. Every morning I only exchange with Him.

"For I have learned how to be content in any circumstance. I know the experience of being in need and of having more than enough; I have learned the secret of being

The Narrow Road

content in any and every circumstance... I can endure all these things through the power of the One who gives me strength." Philippians 4:11-13

I have learned how to be content. There is not anything I need that Jesus cannot give me. I use the list of qualities we made to help me be content when there are forks in the road. I want to be an imitator of Christ where ever I go. Those qualities help me endure every circumstance that comes my way.

I can endure because I love. I can endure because I am compassionate. I can endure because I choose kindness. I can endure because I choose joy. It is His power within me that gives me the strength to choose those things. My Father is constantly teaching me right from wrong, and only *right* leads me to Him. I do not ever want to be on a road that leads me away from my Father. If you were to see my life, I would want it to be easy for you to see where my feet walk.

"You can enter God's Kingdom only through the narrow gate..." Matthew 7:13

I know one day the Narrow Road will come to an end. On that day, I long for my Heavenly Father to be proud of my journey. I am fully convinced that at the end of the Road I am walking, there my Dad waits — He waits just for me. He is The Treasure I have waited for, The Treasure I have walked this Narrow Road for. And guess what?! He feels the same way about me! I am His treasure! I am the one He walked the Narrow Road for. I get overwhelmed knowing that He loves me that much! I hope you feel the same way. With that kind of excitement in our hearts, how can anyone blame us for the passion with which we walk this Road? I am thankful for the past lessons I have learned, the present joy of sharing them with you, and the future I have in Him.

Now I know better; now...I walk better.

> "But small is the Gate and narrow the Road that leads to LIFE, and only a few will find it."
>
> MATTHEW 7:14

ABOUT THE AUTHOR

MacKenzie Myers is the co-owner of Fuzion Studio and Zion Dance Company. She has the great joy of partnering with her sister in these businesses. MacKenzie is the Director of the studio and dance company. She also teaches classes and dances as a member of the company. She is married to Benjamin and has two beautiful daughters, Hannah-Brooke and Judah-Grace. The Myers family of four is passionate about Jesus and shining His light all around the world. MacKenzie's parents and siblings have been her best friends her whole life, and ministering as a family is one of her dearest treasures. Although she takes great joy in her family, friends, job, goofing off, dancing, and singing, MacKenzie lives every day showing us that Jesus is the most important thing in her life.

If you were blessed by *The Narrow Road* and would like to connect with MacKenzie, please do so through one of the options below. She would love to speak with you or simply keep you updated on the adventures of the Myers family.

FACEBOOK: www.facebook.com/mackenzieatheart
INSTAGRAM: @mackenzieatheart
BLOG: www.mackenzieatheart.com
EMAIL: mackenzieatheart@gmail.com

Made in the USA
Middletown, DE
12 May 2015